How to Make a Baby Quilt

Choosing the Fabric

Whether you choose to make your quilt using the traditional method or the new faster methods, you must start by choosing your fabric.

Old time quilts were traditionally made of 100% cotton, and this is still the fabric that experienced quilters prefer.

Cotton has a number of properties that make it especially suitable for patchwork. You will find less distortion with cotton fabric which means that your carefully cut small pieces will fit together more easily. If you make a mistake and find a puckered area, a quilt made of 100% cotton often can be ironed flat with a steam iron. In addition, the needle moves through cotton with ease as opposed to some synthetics. If you are piecing a quilt by hand, or if you are hand quilting, this is an extremely valuable quality.

Instructions for each of our quilts will tell you how much fabric to purchase. Our fabric requirements tend to be rather ample; you may be able to conserve fabric by cutting more carefully.

Many quiltmakers today are omitting the prewashing of fabric to purposely give quilts the puckered look of an antique quilt after it has been washed. This is a fine idea if you are making a quilt which will be entered in a quilt competition or hung on a wall. However, if you are making a quilt for a child, you know that the quilt will need to live through many, many washings. So right from the beginning you want to make sure that you eliminate any future problems.

Therefore, before you begin to work on your quilt, be sure to wash your fabric to check that it is colorfast and preshrunk (don't trust those manufacturers' labels). Test for colorfastness by washing in fairly hot water. Be especially wary of reds and dark blues; they have a tendency to bleed if the initial dyeing was not carefully done. Fabrics which continue to bleed after they have been washed several times should be eliminated.

Make sure your fabric is absolutely square. If it is not, you will have difficulty cutting square pieces. Fabric is woven with crosswise and lengthwise threads. Lengthwise threads should be parallel to the selvage (that's the finished edge along the sides; sometimes the fabric company prints its name along the selvage), and crosswise threads should be perpendicular to the selvage, **Fig 1**. If fabric is off-grain, you can straighten it. Pull gently on the true bias in the opposite direction to the off-grain edge, **Fig 2**. Continue doing this until crosswise threads are at a right angle to lengthwise threads.

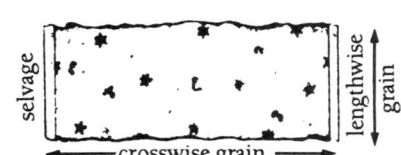

Fig 1

Fig 2

Traditional Piecing

In traditional piecing, each small patch of the quilt block is cut out and then sewn together.

Templates

In quilting, patterns used to cut out patches are called "templates". The patterns for the necessary templates for each quilt are given full size and appear with the specific quilt. To make templates, lay a piece of tracing paper over the pattern pieces in the book and carefully trace the pattern pieces. (Do not photocopy the pieces instead of tracing. Photocopy machines are not exact, and your pieces may not fit together.) Carefully glue your tracing onto heavy cardboard or plastic. Special plastic for making templates is available in quilt, craft or stationery stores. If you use a clear plastic, you can trace directly onto plastic and eliminate the gluing. Now, cut out the plastic or cardboard templates.

It is important that all templates be cut out carefully because if they are not accurate, the patchwork will not fit together. Use a pair of good-size sharp scissors (not the same scissors that you use to cut fabric), a single-edged razor blade or a craft knife. Be careful not to bend the corners of triangles.

Cutting the Pieces

Cutting the fabric is one of the most important steps in making a patchwork block. You must be accurate in order to have the pattern fit smoothly.

Start by laying your laundered, freshly-ironed fabric on a smooth surface with wrong side up. Have all your supplies ready: scissors, rulers, sharp pencils, marking tools, templates, etc.

Whether you choose to piece by hand or machine, cut and piece a trial block first. This will give you a chance to double-check the pattern and to make certain that you like both design and colors.

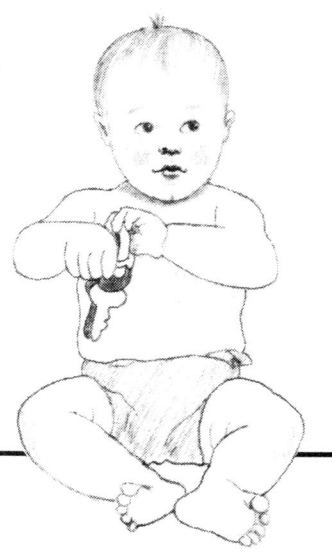

Cutting for Hand Sewing

Lay the cardboard or plastic template on the wrong side of the fabric near top left edge of material (but not on selvage), placing it so that as many straight sides of piece as possible are parallel to crosswise and lengthwise grain of fabric, **Fig 3**. Try

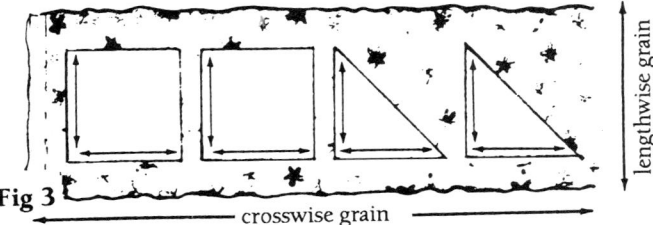
Fig 3

to keep long side of triangles on true bias by placing short sides of triangles on straight of fabric. Trace around template. You can mark with a regular well-sharpened hard lead pencil (using a light color for dark fabrics and a regular pencil for light fabrics), but there are many quilt makers who use fabric marking pens available at quilt stores and departments. Test any marking materials to make certain that they will not run when wet.

Hold your pencil or marker at an angle so that the point is against the side of the template and trace around the template. Measure 1/4" around this shape, and draw a line. This is the line you will cut on. Now you will see that the first line (where you traced your template) is your stitching line. If your cutting line is not perfectly accurate, it will not matter. Your stitching line, however, must be perfectly straight or true, or the pieces will not fit together correctly. In **Fig 4**, the broken line is the cutting line; the solid line is the seam line.

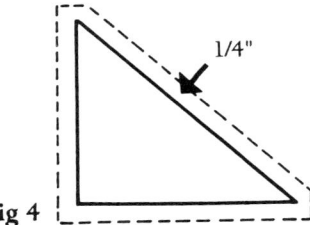
Fig 4

Continue moving template and tracing it on fabric required number of times, moving from left to right and always keeping straight lines parallel with grain. You will save fabric if you have pieces share a common cutting line as in **Fig 5**, but if this is confusing, leave a narrow border or margin around each piece. Use a sharp scissors and cut carefully.

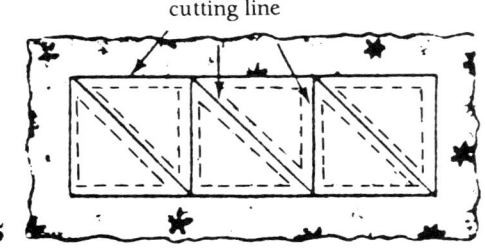
Fig 5

Cutting for Machine Sewing

For machine piecing, an exact 1/4" seam allowance must be measured and marked. Lay the template on the fabric as described above for hand piecing and trace around it with the marking tool, if desired. Now measure the 1/4" seam allowance around this shape. Using a ruler, draw this second line **absolutely accurately**. This is the line that you cut on.

Sewing the Block

Before starting to sew a block, lay out all of the pieces that will be needed for that block. Always work with well-ironed fabric.

Sewing the Block by Machine

Machine piecing is done with the straight stitch foot and throat plate on the machine. Set your machine for about 10 stitches to the inch and use a size 14 needle. The traditional seam allowance in quilting is 1/4" so you are going to need some method to make sure that you sew with a perfect 1/4" seam. If your machine has the 1/4" marked on the throat plate you are in luck. If not, measure 1/4" from your needle hole to the right side of the presser foot and place a piece of tape on the plate. Keep edge of your piece lined up with tape and you will be able to sew a perfect 1/4" seam.

Place two pieces together with right sides facing. Make certain that the top edges of both pieces are even. Pin; baste if desired.

You can construct blocks using the production line method. In this method, **Fig 6**, you do not begin and end your thread with each patch, but let thread run over a continuous chain of patches. When you have made a row of patches, snip them apart. Don't worry about threads coming undone. They will eventually be anchored by the cross seams.

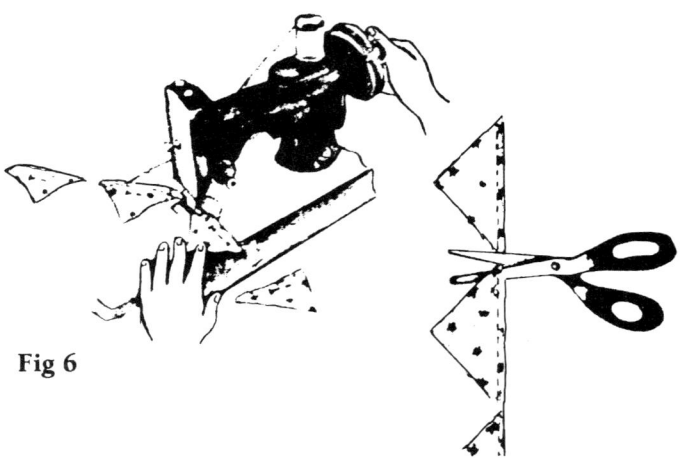
Fig 6

After you have joined two pieces together, press seams flat to one side, not open. Open seams will weaken the quilt. Generally seams can all be pressed in the same direction. But avoid pressing darker pieces so they fall under lighter pieces, since they may show through when quilt is completed.

You may want to turn seam on top in one direction and seam on bottom in opposite direction, **Fig 7**. This will help to keep seams that are crossed with other seams from bunching at crossing points. You can clip away any excess fabric at these points if necessary. Just be sure to iron all seams before they are crossed with another seam. When crossing seams, be especially careful to match seam to seam.

Fig 7

> Hint: As you sew, be careful of fabric's tendency to stretch. This is especially true along bias edges, such as long sides of triangles. Sewing machines are not infallible. Some constantly fight to stretch top fabric. You can learn to win. You may be forced to ease top fabric while stretching bottom fabric on some seams. It helps if you try to feed fabric through machine with grain straight at all times. Be especially careful of stretching bias seam allowances. Whenever possible, sew from large end to pointed end of a piece, and always iron in direction of grain.

Sewing the Block by Hand

Place two pieces together with right sides facing, and place a pin through both pieces at each end of pencil line, **Fig 8**. Check the back to make sure that the pins are exactly on pencil lines. When sewing larger seams, place pins every 1 1/2", removing the pins as you sew past them. Always stitch on the sewing line, being careful not to stitch into the margins at the corners, **Fig 9**. Use a fairly short needle, #7 to #10 (#9 and #10 are the most popular) and no more than an 18" length of thread. Join pieces with short, simple running stitches, taking a few back stitches at the beginning and end of each seam rather than a knot. If the seam is very long, it is a good idea to make a few back stitches at various places along the seam. Take small, evenly spaced stitches and keep the seam as straight as possible along the pencil line. When you sew two bias edges together (as in sewing two triangles along the long side) try to keep the thread taut enough so that the edges do not stretch as you sew them.

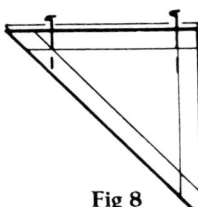
Fig 8

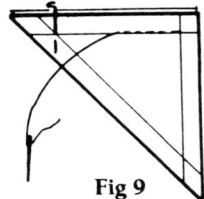
Fig 9

After you have joined the pieces, press the seams as described for machine sewing.

Modern Piecing

The introduction of the rotary cutter has literally revolutionized the art of quilt making. By using a cutter and its accompanying protective mat along with acrylic rulers, you can almost eliminate use of templates. In addition, time spent cutting and piecing can be literally cut in half.

The method usually begins with chain piecing strips and then cutting the strips into squares which are sewn together quickly to create the block.

We have given you explicit instructions for using the newer methods wherever they are applicable. Not every quilt can be made using these methods; for some quilts only part of the work can be done this way.

Some of the techniques which we have listed for the traditional method are still valuable for the modern method. For instance, the 1/4" seam allowance is always used, and pressing seams to one side is still viable.

Blocking the Blocks

When you have completed a block (whether by the traditional or modern method) it must be "blocked" before it is joined to another block. The term "blocking" means keeping the edges straight on all sides of the quilt so it will be a perfect rectangle when finished. The term applies to the quilt's parts as well as to an entire quilt, so the blocking process is a continuous one from start to finish.

Place completed block on the ironing board and pull edges straight with your fingers. Cover block with damp cloth and steam with warm iron (or use steam iron). Iron block perfectly flat with no puckers starting with edges first and center last. Move iron as little as possible to keep block from stretching.

Joining the Blocks

After you have pieced and blocked the required number of blocks for your quilt, lay them out to get the final effect before setting them together.

Using the 1/4" seam allowance, join the blocks in horizontal or vertical rows. When horizontal or vertical rows are completed, join two rows together, matching seam lines. Then add additional rows.

> Hint: When crossing seams, be especially careful to match seam to seam. One learns to do this fairly accurately while sewing by feeling with fingers. It helps if the lower seam is turned one way and the top seam the other, so press seams for odd numbered rows in one direction; even numbered rows in the other.

Adding Borders

Although we give measurements for border strips, we recommend that before cutting your border strips, you measure the quilt top and cut your borders to the actual size. If you have made some mistakes in the piecing (for instance, if you made your blocks with a larger than 1/4" seam allowance) this will be the time to adjust your measurements.

(continued)

Using the 1/4" seam allowance, attach one side border to the right side of the quilt and one to the left. Then attach the top and bottom borders. Use the 1/4" seam allowance at all times. Repeat if attaching additional borders.

Preparing the Quilt Top

Give the quilt top a final blocking, making sure all corners are square and all seams are pressed to one side.

We have made suggestions for quilting your quilt top, but you may wish to follow your own quilting plan. However you are planning to quilt your top, you will need to mark the quilting pattern before joining the top to the backing and batting.

If you prefer to tie your quilt, skip the next section on marking the quilting design.

Marking the Quilting Design

Mark all quilting lines on the **right** side of fabric. For marking, use a hard lead pencil, chalk or other special quilt marking materials. If you quilt right on marked lines, they will not show. Be sure to test any marking material to find one that works best for you.

If you are merely quilting around the patchwork pieces, you may not need to mark your line if you feel that you can accurately gauge the 1/4" line as you work. If you are quilting "in the ditch" of the seam (the space right in the seam), marking is not necessary. Other quilting patterns will need to be marked.

Attaching Batting and Backing

There are a number of different types of batting on the market. Thin batting will require a great deal of quilting to hold it (quilting lines no more than 1" apart); very thick batting can be used **only** for tied quilts.

For most quilt projects, you are probably better off with a medium weight bonded polyester sheet batting.

We have indicated the amount of fabric required for the backing in each pattern. If you prefer another fabric, buy a backing fabric that is soft and loosely woven so that the quilting needle can pass through easily. Bed sheets are usually not good backing materials.

If your quilt is wider than the available fabric, you will have to sew lengths together to make your quilt backing. Cut off selvages and seam pieces together carefully; iron seam open. **This is the only time in making a quilt that a seam should be pressed open.**

Cut batting and backing larger than the quilt top: about 2" wider on all sides than quilt top. Place backing, wrong side up, on flat surface. Place batting on top of this, matching outer edges. The layers can be basted together with thread or safety pins. **For thread basting**, first pin backing and batting together; then baste with long stitches, starting in center and sewing toward edges in a number of diagonal lines. Now center quilt top, right side up on top of batting. Baste top to batting and backing layers in same manner. **For safety pin basting**, layer backing, batting and top and pin through all three layers at once. Start pinning from the center and work out to the edges, placing pins 4" - 6" apart, avoiding your quilting lines. Choose rustproof pins that are size #1 or #2.

Hand Quilting

The actual quilting stitch is really a fairly simple one for anyone who has ever sewn. There are many books which attempt to teach the quilter how to make the proper stitch. It's something like teaching someone to swim with a swimming manual. You're never really going to learn unless you dive right into the water!

The stitch is just a very simple running stitch, but working through three layers at once may be a bit difficult at first. Use one of the short, fine needles especially designed for quilting (they are often called "betweens"), and 100% cotton quilting thread.

By the way, all quilters wear thimbles! If you have never used a thimble before, you are going to have to now. The thimble is worn on the middle finger of your right hand (or your left, if you are left-handed). The thimble is used to push the needle through the fabric as in **Fig 10**.

Fig 10

The quilting can be done in a traditional floor frame, but chances are you'll probably find a quilting hoop more convenient. Place hoop over middle of quilt, pull quilt slightly taut (not as stretched as for embroidery) and move extra fullness toward edges. Begin working in center and move extra fullness toward outer edges. As you work, you will find the quilting stitch has a tendency to push batting, and by working from center out you can gradually ease any excess fullness toward edges. If you wish, run quilting thread through beeswax to keep it from tangling.

Begin with an 18" length of thread with a knot in one end. Go into quilt through top about 1/2" from where you plan to begin quilting, and bring needle up to quilting line. Pull gently but firmly, and knot will slip through the batting where it will disappear. Now place left hand under hoop where needle should come through. With right hand push needle vertically downward through layers of the quilt until it touches left hand.

If you are a beginner, you may need to pull needle through with left hand, and push it back upward to where it is received by right hand, close to last stitch. As you become more proficient, you will be able to do the whole operation with one hand, merely using the left hand to signal that the needle has penetrated the three layers. Some experienced quilters are able to put several stitches on the needle just as if they were sewing.

Make stitches as close together as you can; this is the real secret of beautiful quilting. The stitches should be evenly spaced, the same length on the front as on the back. When entire quilt has been quilted, lift it from frame or hoop and remove basting stitches.

Machine Quilting

Many of the quilts photographed in this book were actually quilted on the sewing machine. Fine transparent nylon thread was used for the top thread, while regular sewing thread was used for the bobbin. The small quilts in this book will need a minimum amount of rolling to fit the quilt under the sewing machine. Start your quilting in the center and work out to the sides.

To **quilt-in-the-ditch** of a seam, use your hands to pull the blocks or pieces apart and machine stitch right between the two pieces. Try to keep your stitching just to the side of the seam that does not have the bulk of the seam allowance under it. When you are finished stitching, the quilting will be practically hidden in the seam.

We have used **straight line machine quilting** next to a seam (as in *Little Red Schoolhouse*) and diagonally through blocks (as in *Trip Around the Playground*). You may want to mark these quilting lines with a ruler. It may take a little practice to feel in control and keep the lines of quilting straight.

Free form machine quilting is done with a darning foot and the feed dogs down on your sewing machine. It can be used to quilt around a design (as in *My Dolly's Tea Party*) or to quilt a motif (as in *Little Irish Leprechaun*). Mark your quilting design as described in Marking the Quilting Design on page 4. Free form machine quilting takes practice to master because **you** are controlling the quilt through the machine rather than the machine moving the quilt. With free form machine quilting you can quilt in any direction—up and down, side to side and even in circles without pivoting the quilt around the needle.

Tying the Quilt

Use knitting worsted weight yarn (washable of course), crochet thread, several strands of embroidery floss or other washable material.

Work from center of quilt out, adjusting any excess fullness of batting as you go. Thread an 18" length of yarn into a large-eyed needle. Do not knot! Take needle down from top through all three layers, leaving about 1" of yarn on right side. Bring needle back up from wrong side to right side, about 1/8" from where needle first entered. Tie a firm knot, then cut, leaving both ends about 1/2" long. Make sufficient ties to keep three layers together.

Attaching the Binding

Place quilt on flat surface and carefully trim backing and batting 1/2" beyond quilt top edge. Measure quilt top and cut two 2"-wide binding strips the length of your quilt (for sides). Right sides together, sew one side strip to one side of quilt with 1/4" seam allowance (seam allowance should be measured from outer edge of quilt top fabric, not outer edge of batting/backing). Turn binding to back and turn under 1/4" on raw edge; slipstitch to backing. Do other side in same manner. For top and bottom edge binding strips, measure carefully adding 1/2" to each end; cut strips 2" wide. To eliminate raw edges at corners, turn the extra 1/2" to wrong side before stitching to top and bottom. Finish in same manner as sides.

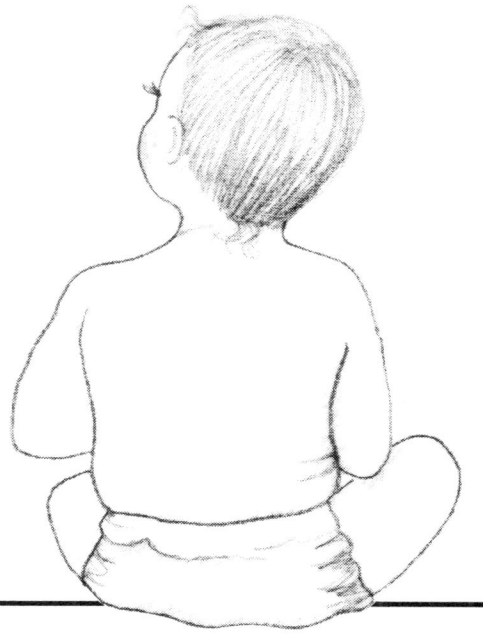

Dinosaur Go-Round
Big Folks' Pattern: Pinwheels

The dinosaurs are on parade, and they are marching right over the quilt while the pinwheels fly in the breeze.

If you have ever wondered how to use those wild fabrics that are currently on the market, here is one answer. You cut out the individual motifs, and use them as blocks for a quilt. In this quilt, we were able to cut out dinosaurs, but you might prefer jungle creatures, or cats, or even giant flowers. It really depends upon what you can find at your local quilt or fabric stores.

Size of Pinwheel Block:
6" x 6"

Size of Dinosaur Block:
6" x 6"

Size of Quilt:
Approx 37 1/2" x 46"

Setting:
The pinwheel blocks are set on point 4 across and 5 down. The Dinosaur Blocks are set between the Pinwheel Blocks with half and quarter blocks created from Templates B and C used to fill out the edges. The quilt is finished with a 1 1/2" border and a 1/4" binding cut from the yellow fabric.

Fabric Requirements:
dinosaur or bold print fabric: Approx 3 yds
red, fuchsia, blue, green fabric: 1/2 yd.
yellow fabric: 3 yds (includes backing and binding)

Fabric Note: You will need 30 dinosaurs (or other animals), so carefully check the fabric to make certain that you can cut that many animals from the fabric.

Traditional Method
Cut the following:

Template A red	32
Template A fuchsia	20
Template A blue	40
Template A green	36
Template A yellow	32
Template B dinosaur fabric	14
Template C dinosaur fabric	4

Dinosaur Blocks:
Cut twelve 6 1/2" x 6 1/2" squares from dinosaur fabric

Side Borders:
Cut two yellow strips each 2" x 43"

Top and Bottom Borders:
Cut two yellow strips each 2" x 37 1/2"

Cutting Note: Since the dinosaur blocks will be set on point, make certain that the blocks are cut with the dinosaur placed pleasingly as in Fig 1.

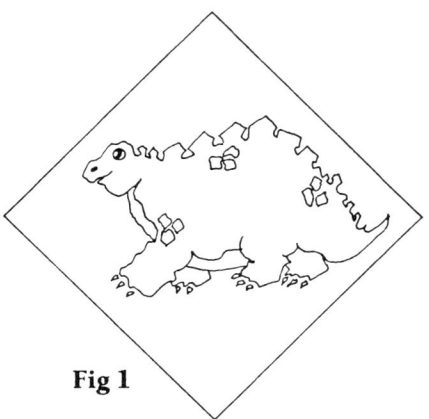

Fig 1

Instructions:

1. Following the pinwheel Block Diagram, make 20 blocks in the following color combinations:

red and blue:	2 blocks
green and yellow:	2 blocks
fuchsia and blue:	3 blocks
fuchsia and green:	2 blocks
blue and yellow:	3 blocks
red and green:	3 blocks
green and blue:	2 blocks
red and yellow:	3 blocks

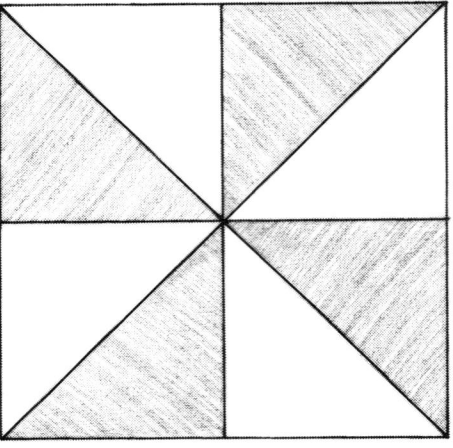

Block Diagram

2. The quilt is constructed in diagonal strips. Follow the diagram in **Fig 2** which shows you exactly how each strip should be made.

3. Join the strips, adding two C triangles at the corners as shown in **Fig 2**.

4. Turn the quilt so that the blocks are on point as in the quilt layout.

5. Add the side borders; then, add the top and bottom borders.

6. To finish quilt, follow instructions in *How to Make a Baby Quilt*, starting with Preparing the Quilt Top on page 4.

For color photograph, see page 23.

Fig 2

(continued)

Dinosaur Go-Round

Modern Method

Cutting Requirements:
three 8 3/4" x 12 3/4" pieces, red
four 8 3/4" x 12 3/4" pieces, blue
four 8 3/4 x 12 3/4" pieces, green
three 8 3/4" x 12 3/4" pieces, yellow
two 8 3/4" x 12 3/4" pieces, fuchsia
twelve 6 1/2" x 6 1/2" squares, dinosaur fabric
fourteen Template B pieces, dinosaur fabric
four Template C pieces, dinosaur fabric
two 2" x 43" strips, yellow
two 2 " x 37 1/2" strips, yellow

Instructions:

1. To make the pieced squares, use the 8 3/4" x 12 3/4" pieces of fabric in the color combinations found in step 1 of the Traditional Method above, and follow these steps:

a. Starting at least 1/2" from all edges of **wrong** side of the lighter piece, draw a grid with lines 3 7/8" apart, being sure that your squares are drawn **accurately**. You will have a grid with 2 squares across and 3 down, **Fig 3**.

b. Draw diagonal lines through every other square, **Fig 4**.

c. Draw diagonal lines in the opposite direction through all of the empty squares, **Fig 5**.

d. Place marked fabric right sides together with corresponding color for the block that you are working on. Press together lightly and pin or baste the two pieces to hold in place. Referring to **Fig 6** and starting in a corner where the diagonal line goes from the outside to the inside, stitch 1/4" to the left of the drawn diagonal line. Continue stitching along the diagonal lines until you reach the corner where you started. Make sure you have stitched on both sides of all diagonal lines.

e. Remove pins or basting and press well. Using scissors or rotary cutter and mat, cut along every marked line—horizontal, vertical, and diagonal. Press each pieced square open with the seam allowance toward the darker side. Clip "dog ears" from each square, **Fig 7**.

f. Repeat with all other color combinations. You will have a total of 12 pieced squares from each color combination for a total of 96; you will need 80 to complete the quilt. (Leftover squares can be used to make a small pillow.)

2. Sew four pieced squares together from one color combination to form Pinwheel Block. See Pinwheel Block Diagram. Repeat with remaining pieced squares until you have a total of 20 for your quilt.

3. Follow steps 2 to 6 of Traditional Method above to complete your quilt.

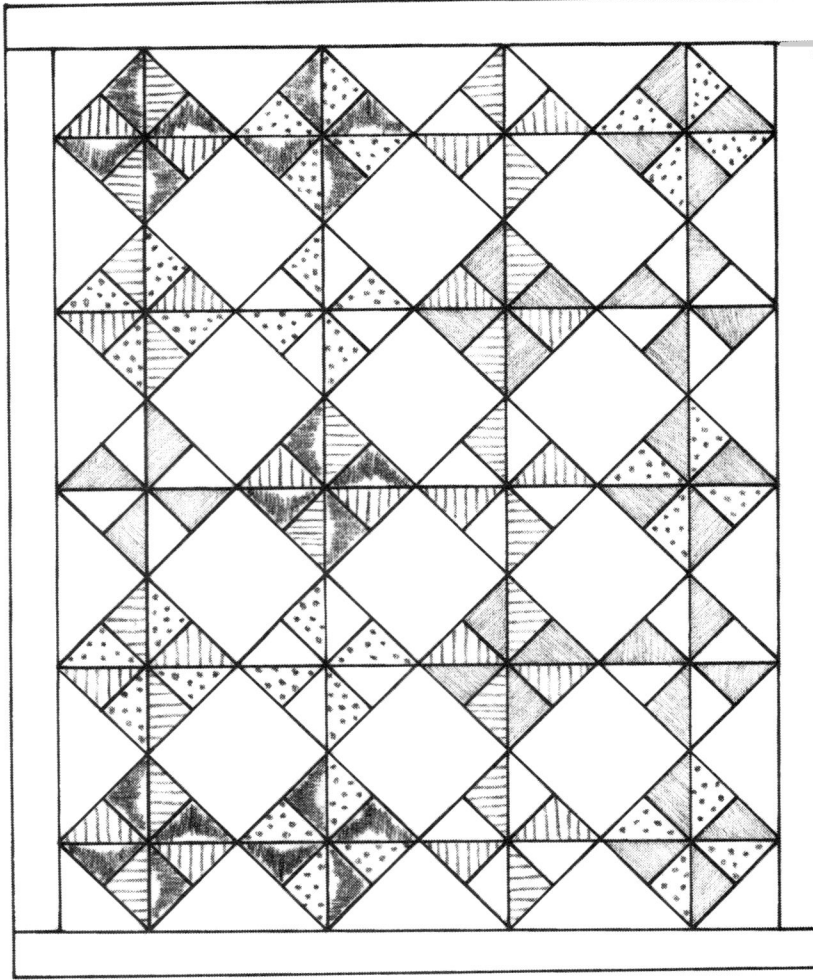

Dinosaur Go-Round Layout

red
fuchsia
blue
green
yellow

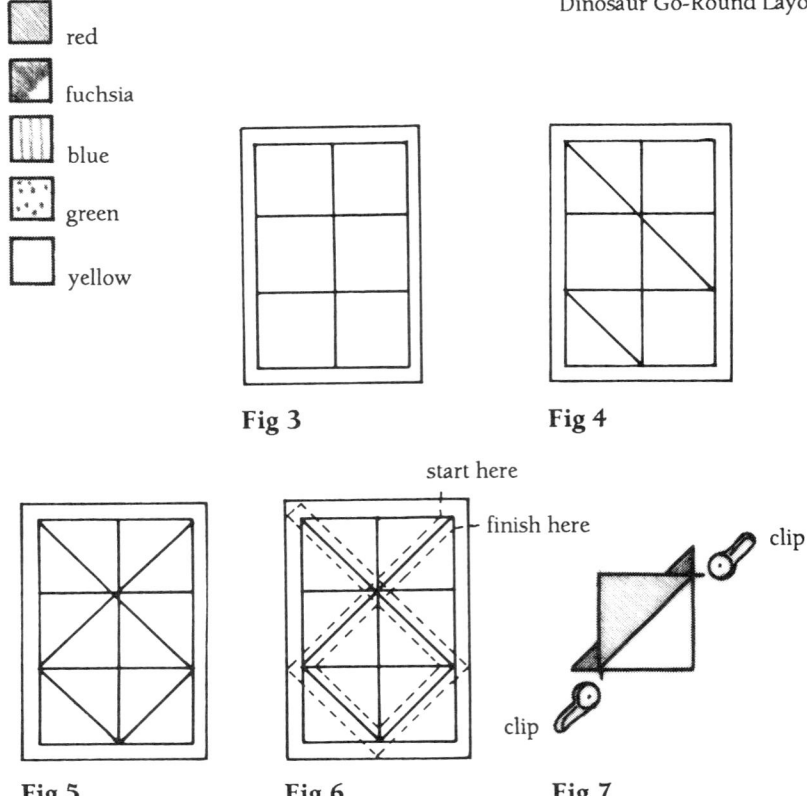

Fig 3   Fig 4

Fig 5   Fig 6   Fig 7

8

Quilting Suggestion:

The quilt shown in the photograph was quilted in the ditch around all of the squares. Bright colored yarn was used to tie the centers of each pinwheel.

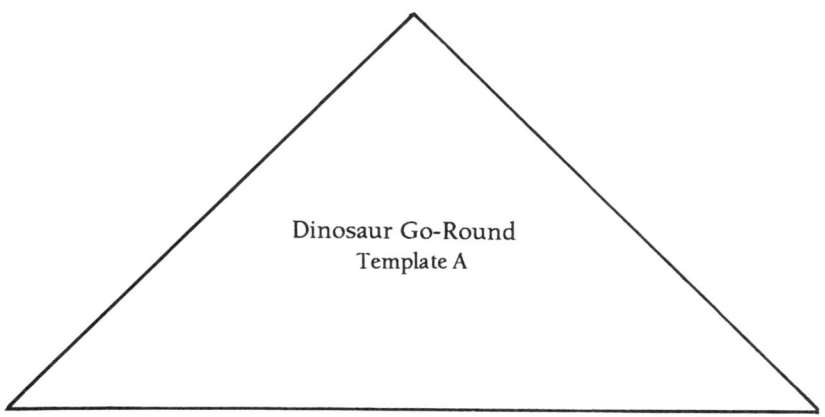

Dinosaur Go-Round
Template A

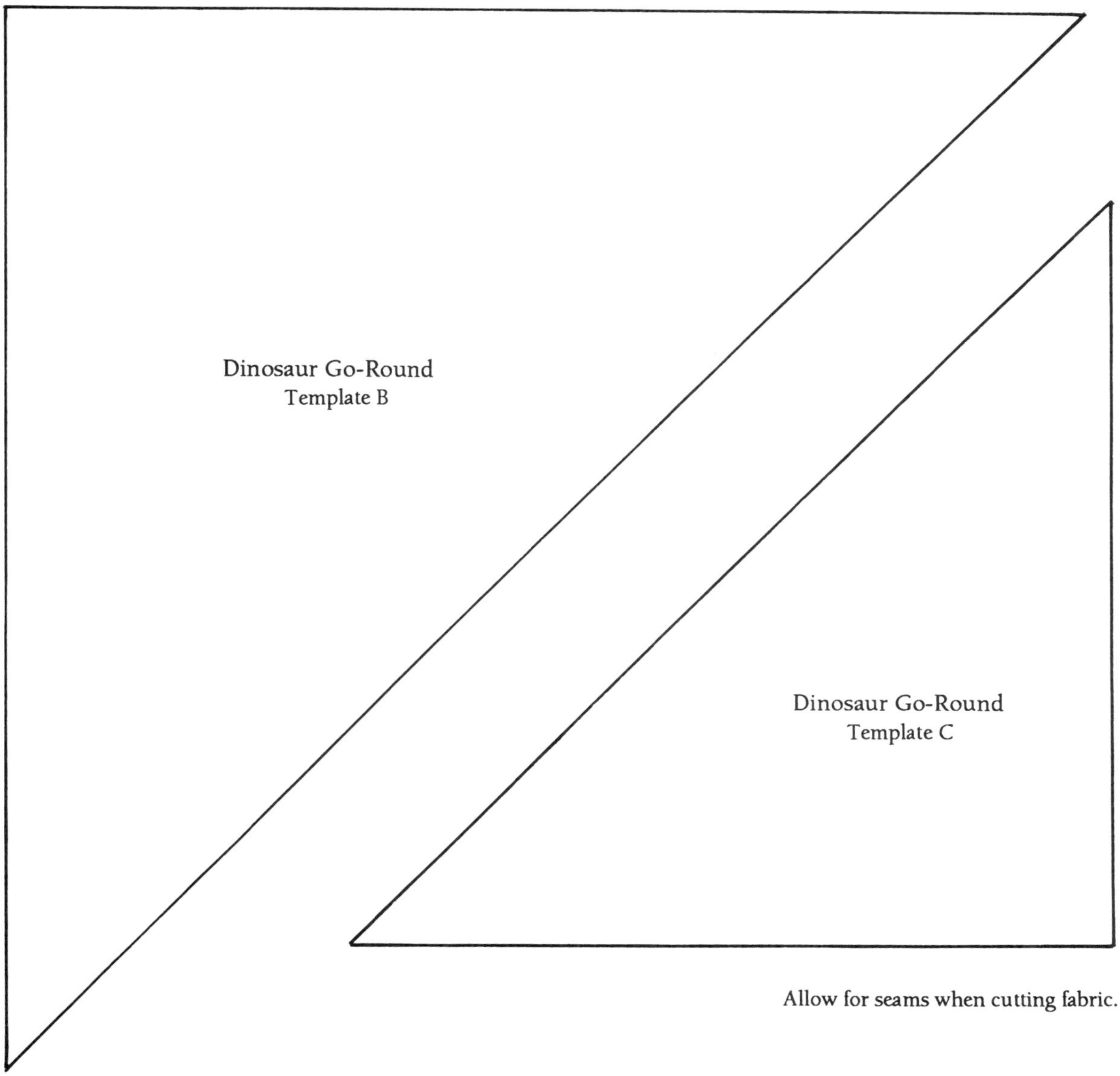

Dinosaur Go-Round
Template B

Dinosaur Go-Round
Template C

Allow for seams when cutting fabric.

My Dolly's Tea Party
Big Folks' Pattern: Nine Patch

The dollies are having a tea party, and they've invited the teddy bears to join them along with Mr. Mouse. Don't they look just wonderful dressed in their Sunday best? The toys that were used in this quilt are part of a printed juvenile novelty fabric. These fabrics come with blocks of motifs printed in panels. If you are unable to locate the exact print that we used in our quilt, you should have no trouble in finding similar printed fabric in your quilt or fabric store. When you purchase the fabric, count the repeats carefully so that you will have a separate motif for each block.

Size of Toy Block:
7" x 7"

Size of Nine Patch Block:
3" x 3"

Size of Quilt:
Approx 34 1/2" x 44 1/2"

Setting:
The toy blocks are set 3 across and 4 down with sashing created from strips of blue print and white print fabrics plus the nine patch blocks. A border is created from the blue print and white print fabrics with nine patch blocks at each corner. The quilt is finished with a 3/4" binding.

Fabric Requirements:
Toy block fabric: Approx 1 yd

Fabric Note: Check the fabric to make certain that you will have enough printed fabric for the 12 blocks.

blue print: 1 1/4 yds
white print: 2 3/4 yds (includes backing and binding)

Traditional Method:
Cut the following:

	for block	for quilt
7 1/2" x 7 1/2" toy fabric	1	12
Template A blue print	4	40
Template A white print	5	50

Sashing Strips:
Cut 17 white print strips, each 7 1/2" x 1 1/2"
Cut 34 blue print strips, each 7 1/2" x 1 1/2"
First Side Borders:
Cut 2 white print strips, each 37 1/2" x 1 1/2"
Cut 4 blue print strips, each 37 1/2 x 1 1/2"
First Top and Bottom Borders:
Cut 2 white print strips, each 27 1/2" x 1 1/2"
Cut 4 blue print strips, each 27 1/2" x 1 1/2"

Second Border:
Cut 2 white print strips, each 3 1/2" x 43 1/2" for sides
Cut 2 white print strips, each 3 1/2" x 40 for top and bottom

Instructions:
1. Make 10 Nine Patch blocks following the Block Diagram.

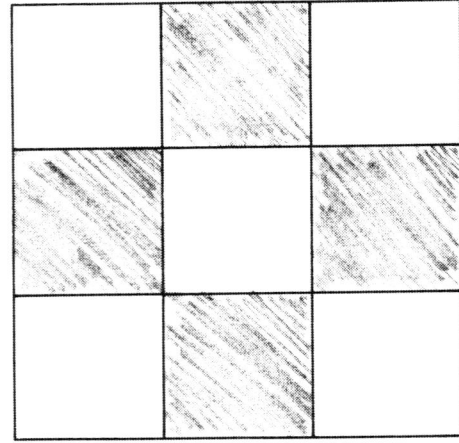

Nine Patch Block Diagram

2. Join blue sashing strips to white sashing strips to make 17 strips, **Fig 1**.

3. Join four Toy Blocks to sashing strips as shown, **Fig 2**. You now have a vertical strip of four joined blocks.

4. Make two more vertical strips.

5. Join three Nine Patch blocks to sashing strips as shown in **Fig 3** to create long sashing strip. Repeat this process for the second long sashing strip.

6. Following **Fig 4**, join the vertical strips to the long sashing strips created in step 5.

Fig 1

Fig 2   Fig 3

Fig 4

7. Create a side border by joining two blue print strips to either side of the white print strip. Repeat the process for the second side border.

8. Following **Fig 5**, join the two side strips to the quilt.

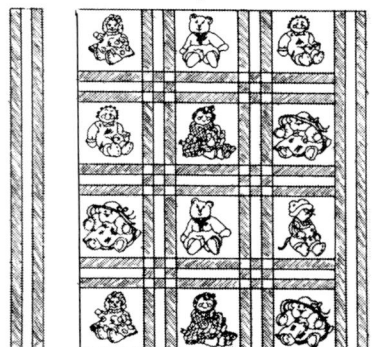

Fig 5

9. Make the top and bottom borders by joining two blue print strips to either side of the white strip. Add two Nine Patch blocks to the sides as in **Fig 6**.

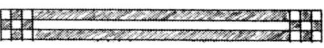

Fig 6

10. Add the top and bottom borders to the quilt as in **Fig 7**.

Fig 7

11. Add the second white print border to the sides of the quilt and then to the top and bottom.

12. To finish quilt, follow instructions in *How to Make a Baby Quilt*, starting with Preparing the Quilt Top on page 4.

For color photograph, see page 21.

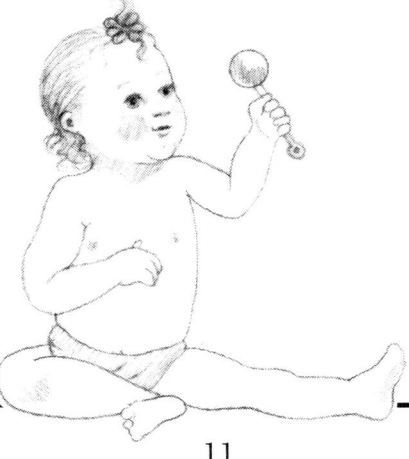

My Dolly's
Tea Party
Template A

Allow for seams when cutting fabric.

(continued)

My Dolly's Tea Party

Modern Method
Cutting Requirements:
7 1/2" x 7 1/2" squares from toy fabric
seven 1 1/2" crosswise strips from white print
eleven 1 1/2" crosswise strips from blue print

Cut Side Borders, Top and Bottom Borders and Second Borders as specified in Traditional Method above.

Instructions:

1. For sashing strips, sew a blue print strip on each long side of a white print strip, **Fig 8**. Repeat with three more sets of strips. Cut crosswise every 7 1/2" until you have 17 pieces, **Fig 9**.

2. For Nine Patch Blocks, sew a blue print strip along each long side of a white print strip for Strip 1; then sew a white print strip on each side of a blue print strip, for Strip 2. Cut crosswise every 1 1/2" until you have ten pieces of Strip 1 and 20 pieces of Strip 2. Sew a Strip 2 piece on each long side of a Strip 1 piece, **Fig 10**, until you have all 10 Nine Patch Blocks.

3. For Border Strips, sew a blue print border strip on each side of a white print border strip. Repeat with other border strip fabrics.

4. Follow steps 2 through 12 of Traditional Method above to complete your quilt.

Quilting Suggestions:
The quilt shown in the photograph was quilted around the toys and in the ditch as shown in **Fig 11**.

My Dolly's Tea Party Layout

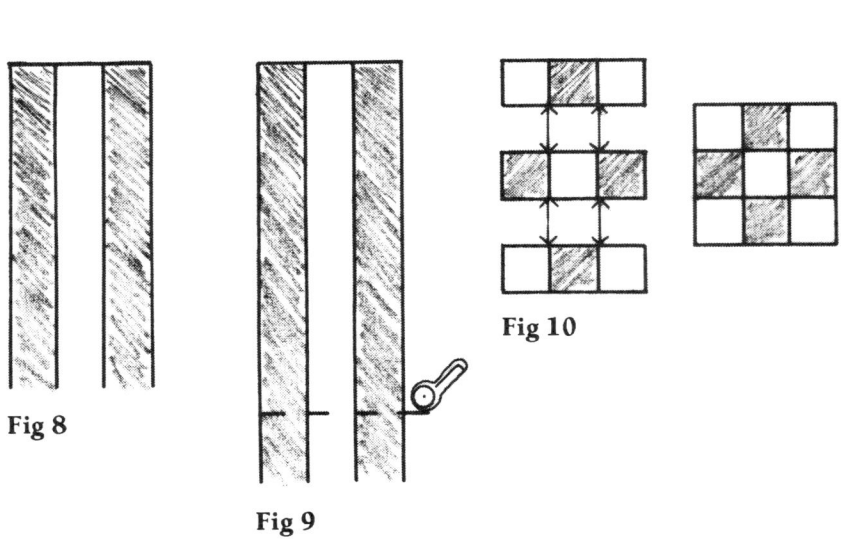

Fig 11 My Dolly's Tea Party Quilting Layout

Log Cabin Playhouse

Big Folks' Pattern: Log Cabin

Take a traditional Log Cabin quilt — one of the most popular ever made — use thin "logs" and pastel colors, and you have made a quilt that any child would love.

Size of Block:
5 1/4" x 5 1/4"

Size of Quilt:
Approx 33" x 43 1/2"

Setting:
The blocks are set 6 across and 8 down with a 3/4" binding.

Fabric Requirements:
blue: 3/4 yds
yellow, blue print, green: 1/2 yd
white print: 1 1/4 yds
(includes backing and binding)
yellow print, pink: 1/4 yd

Traditional Method
Cut the following:

	for block	for quilt
Template A white print	1	48
Template A pink	1	48
Template B yellow print	2	96
Template C pink	1	48
Template C blue print	1	48
Template D yellow	2	96
Template E blue print	1	48
Template E blue	1	48
Template F green	2	96
Template G blue	1	48

Instructions:

1. Make 48 blocks following the Block Diagram, **Fig 1**.

2. Join the blocks following the quilt layout. Be especially careful that each block is turned correctly.

3. To finish quilt, follow instructions in *How to Make a Baby Quilt*, starting with Preparing the Quilt Top on page 4.

(continued)

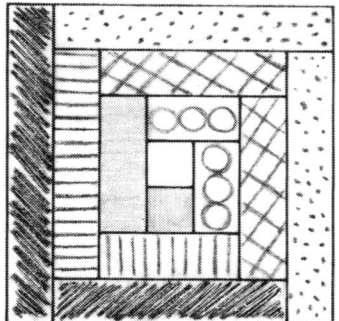

Fig 1   Block Diagram

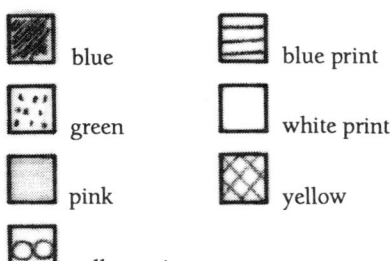

blue
green
pink
yellow print
blue print
white print
yellow

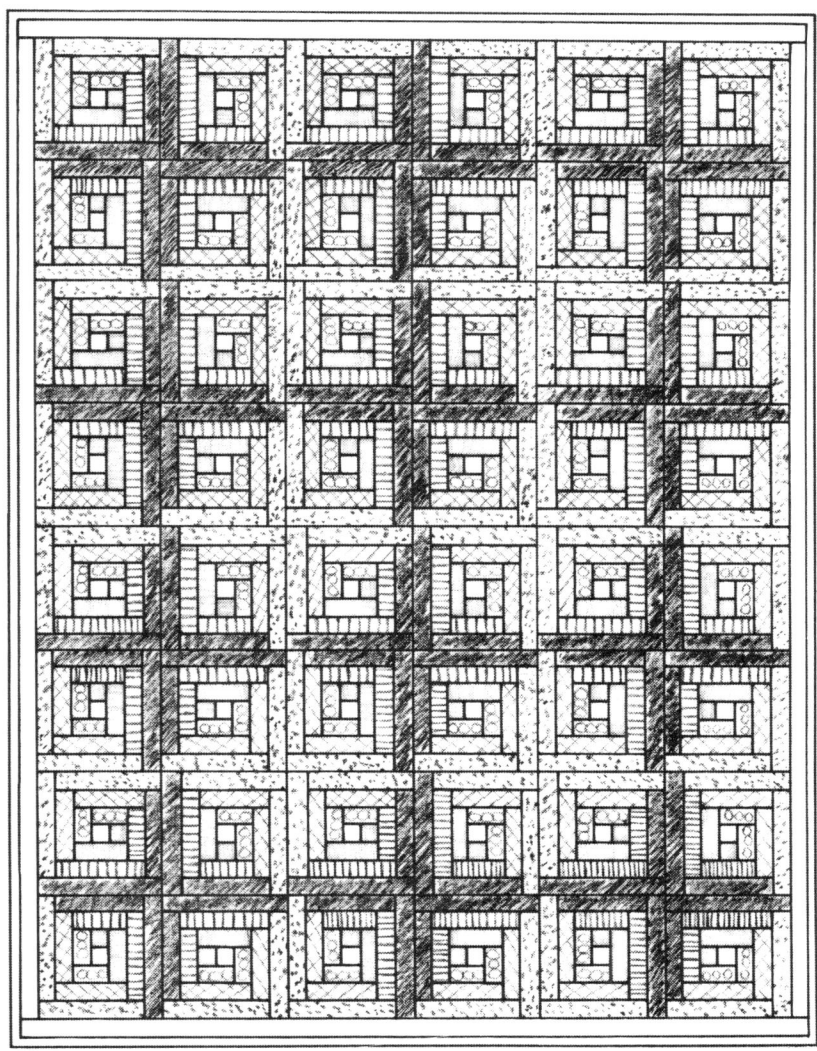

Log Cabin Playhouse Layout

(continued)

Log Cabin Playhouse

Modern Method

You will be making 48 unit blocks, **Fig 1**, using the chain-piecing method.

Cutting Requirements:

two	1 1/2" strips, white print (Strip 1)
five	1 1/2" strips, pink (Strips 2 and 5)
five	1 1/2" strips, yellow print (Strips 3 and 4)
nine	1 1/2" strips, blue print (Strips 6 and 9)
nine	1 1/2" strips, yellow (Strips 7 and 8)
thirteen	1 1/2" strips, blue (Strips 10 and 13)
thirteen	1 1/2" strips, green (Strips 11 and 12)

Instructions:

1. Sew one white print strip and one pink strip together; repeat. Press seam toward pink. Cut crosswise every 1 1/2" until you have 48 piece 1-2, **Fig 2**.

2. Turn piece 1-2 a quarter turn in a clockwise direction and begin chain-piecing by stitching piece 1-2 to Strip 3. Continue chain-piecing all 48 pieces, **Fig 3**. Cut Strip 3 even with length of piece 1-2. Press seam away from center.

3. Turn piece 1-2-3 a quarter turn in a clockwise direction and add Strip 4, chain-piecing all 48 pieces. Cut and press as in Step 2.

4. Continue turning and chain-piecing Strips 5 through 13, **Fig 5**, until all 48 blocks are completed.

5. Follow steps 2 and 3 of Traditional Method above to complete your quilt.

Quilting Suggestion:

The photographed quilt was quilted with diagonal squares as indicated in **Fig 6**.

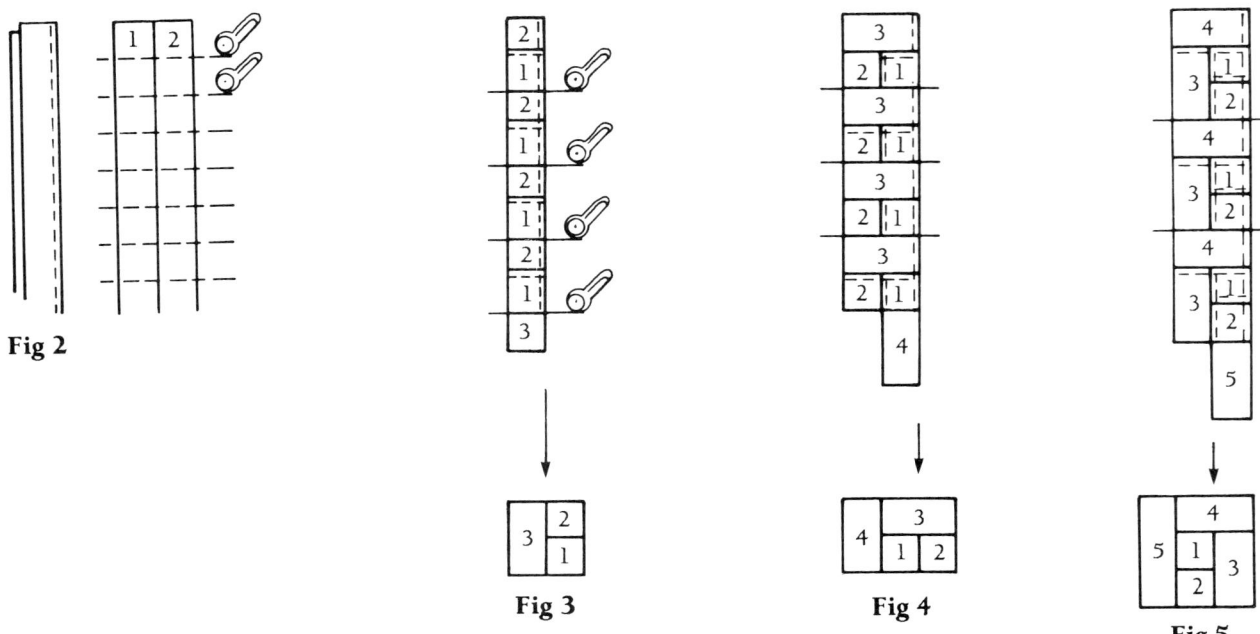

Fig 2   Fig 3   Fig 4   Fig 5

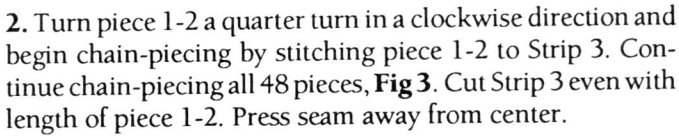

Log Cabin Playhouse
Template G

Log Cabin Playhouse
Template F

Allow for seams when cutting fabric.

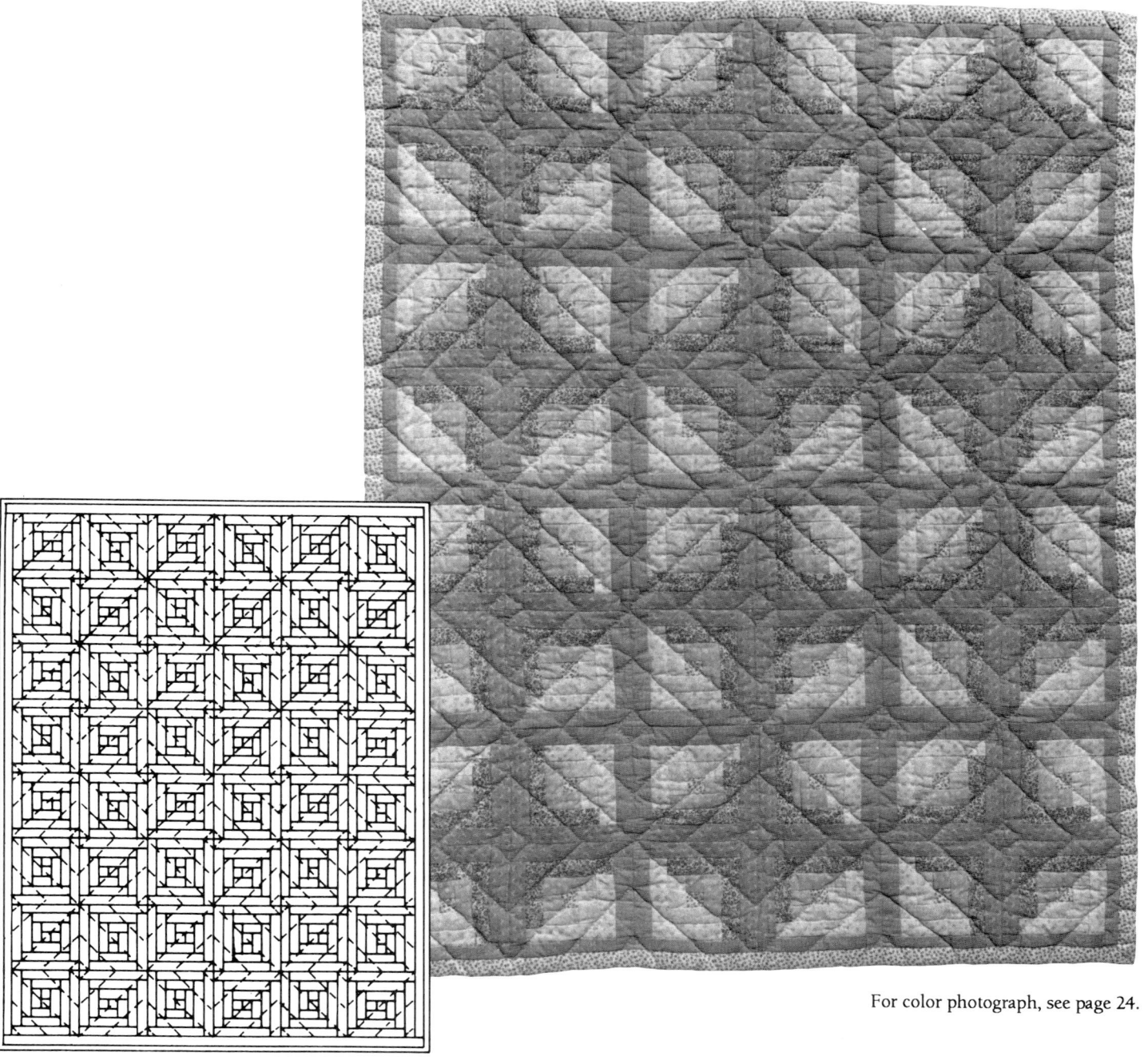

For color photograph, see page 24.

Fig 6 Log Cabin Playhouse Quilting Layout

Log Cabin Playhouse
Template E

Log Cabin Playhouse
Template D

Log Cabin
Playhouse
Template C

Allow for seams when cutting fabric.

Log Cabin
Playhouse
Template B

Log Cabin
Playhouse
Template A

Little Red Schoolhouse

Big Folks' Pattern: Little Red Schoolhouse

Grandmother may very well have gone to a little red schoolhouse that looked like the ones in this quilt. Perhaps that's why the quilt block has been around for such a long time. Most little tykes today will never go to such a charming little red schoolhouse; so why not keep the memory alive on a quilt? We used four different reds to create our schools; you may remember your schoolhouse as being only one red.

Size of Block:
9" x 9"

Size of Quilt:
Approx 43 1/2" x 52 1/2"

Setting:
The blocks are set 4 across and 5 down with a 1" border of the natural fabric and a 2" border of one of the red print fabrics. The quilt is finished with a 3/4" binding of the same red fabric as the border.

Fabric Requirements:

red print 1, 2 and 4:	3/4 yd
red print 3:	2 1/2 yds (includes border, backing and binding)
natural:	1 1/2 yds

Traditional Method
Cut the following:

	for block	for quilt
Template A red print 1	2	10
Template A red print 2	2	10
Template A red print 3	2	10
Template A red print 4	2	10
Template B natural	1	20
Template C red print 1	1	5
Template C red print 2	1	5
Template C red print 3	1	5
Template C red print 4	1	5
Template D red print 1	2	10
Template D red print 2	2	10
Template D red print 3	2	10
Template D red print 4	2	10
Template D natural	1	20
Template E red print 1	3	15
Template E red print 2	3	15
Template E red print 3	3	15
Template E red print 4	3	15
Template E natural	2	40
Template F natural	1	20
Template G natural	1	20
Template H red print 1	1	5
Template H red print 2	1	5
Template H red print 3	1	5
Template H red print 4	1	5
Template I red print 1	1	5
Template I red print 2	1	5
Template I red print 3	1	5
Template I red print 4	1	5
Template J natural	1	20
Template K natural	1	20
Template L natural	1	20
Template M red print 1	2	10
Template M red print 2	2	10
Template M red print 3	2	10
Template M red print 4	2	10
Template N natural	1	20
Template O natural	1	20

First Border:
Cut 2 natural strips each 1 1/2" x 45 1/2" for sides
Cut 2 natural strips each 1 1/2" x 38 1/2" for top and bottom

Second Border:
Cut 2 red print 3 strips each 2 1/2" x 47 1/2" for sides
Cut 2 red print 3 strips each 2 1/2" x 45 1/2" for top and bottom

Instructions:

1. Make five blocks of each of the four red prints following the Block Diagram.

2. Join the blocks following the Quilt Layout, and placing the red print schools as shown in **Fig 1**.

3. Add the natural borders and then the borders made from the red print 3 fabric.

4. To finish quilt, follow instructions in *How to Make a Baby Quilt*, starting with Preparing the Quilt Top on page 4.

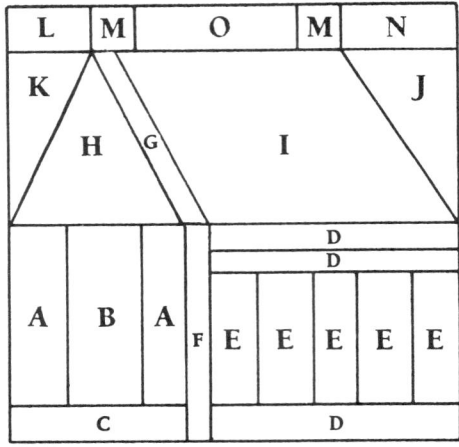

Block Diagram

For color photograph, see back cover.

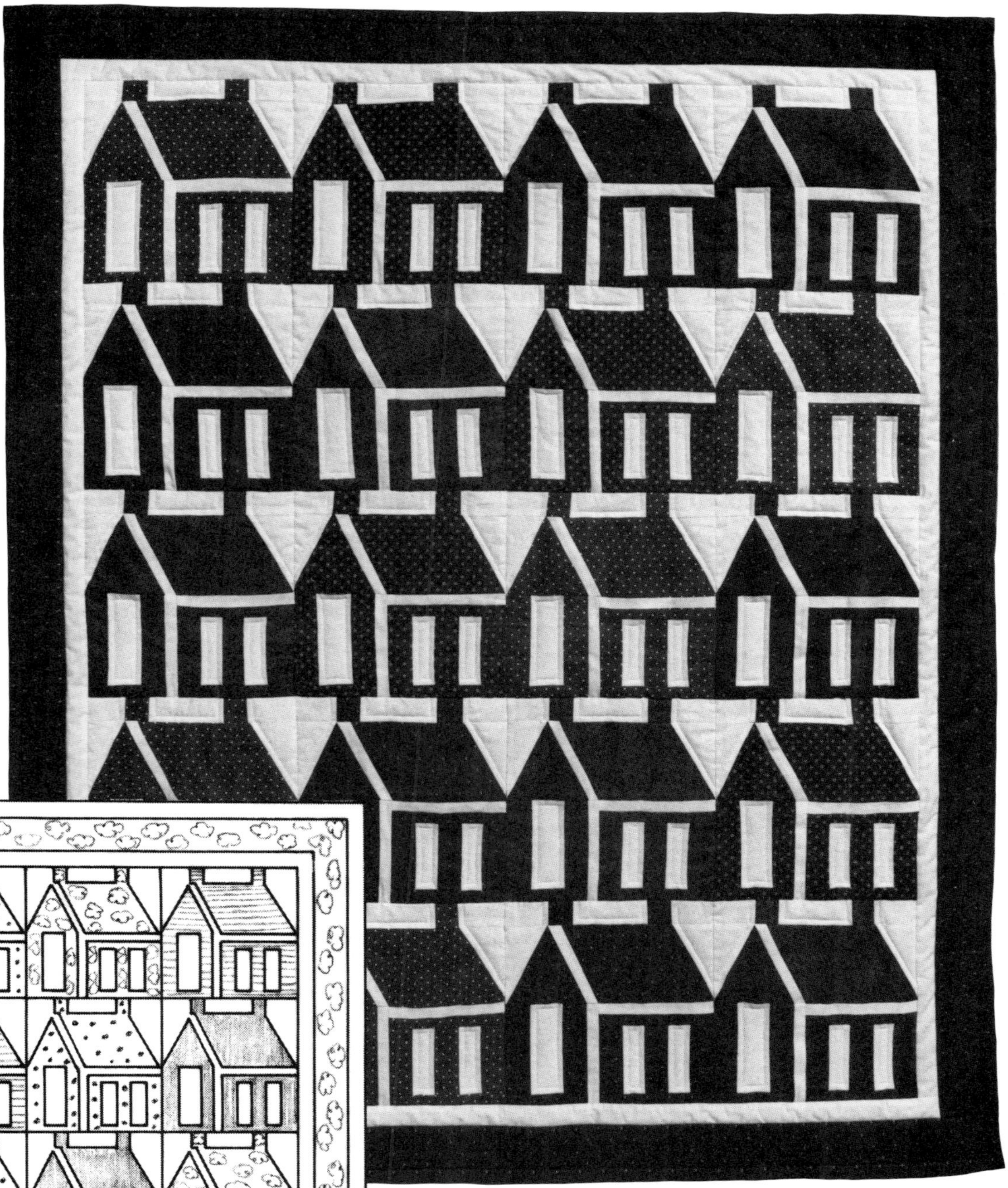

red print 1
red print 2
red print 3
red print 4

Little Red Schoolhouse Layout

1 2 3 4
3 4 2 1
4 2 1 3
1 3 4 2
2 1 3 4

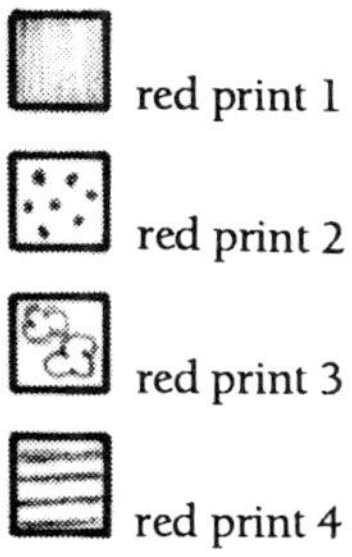

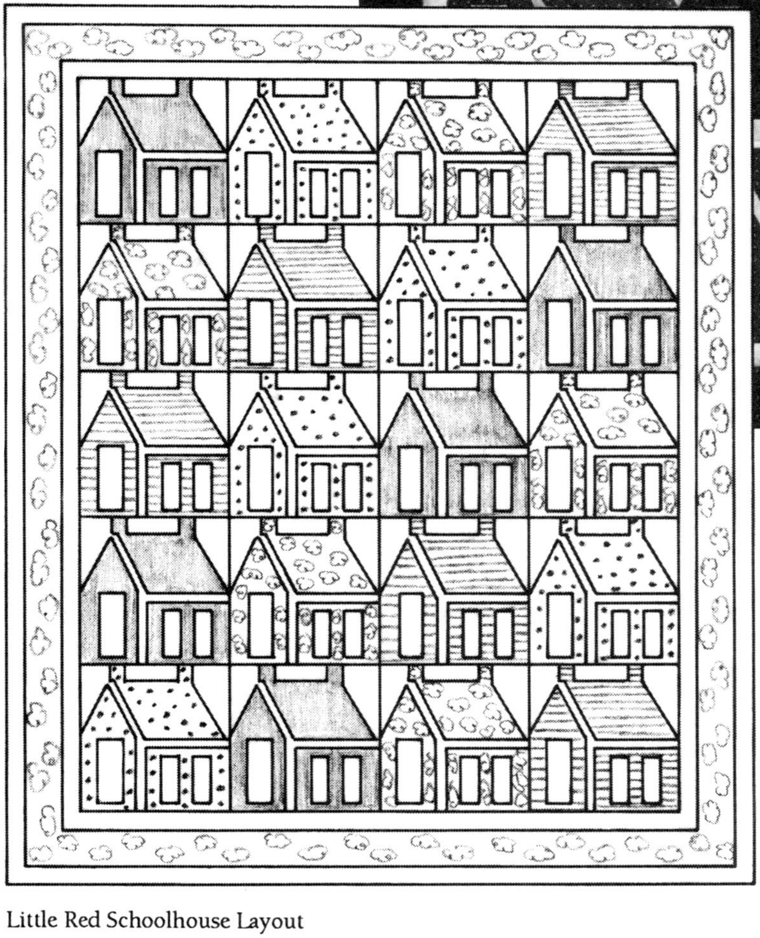

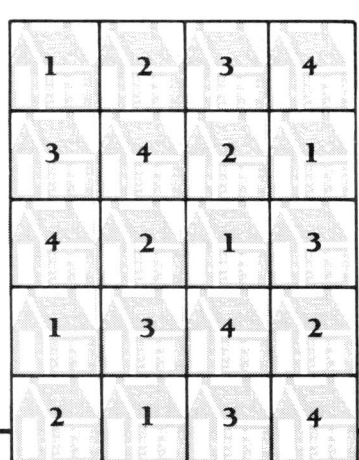

Fig 1

(continued)

Little Red Schoolhouse

Modern Method

You can take advantage of strip piecing techniques to save several steps in making the blocks. Be sure to use the same print throughout each block.

Blocks are made in three sections as shown in Block Diagram, page 16.

Cutting Requirements:

four	2 1/4" x 9" strips, natural
four	2 1/2" x 9" strips, natural
eight	1 1/2" x 9" strips, each red print (1, 2, 3 and 4)
four	1 1/2" strips, natural
four	3 3/4" x 9" strips, natural
twelve	2 " strips, natural
four	1" strip, natural
three	1" strips, each red print (1, 2, 3 and 4)
five	Template C pieces, each red print (1, 2, 3 and 4)
five	Template D pieces, each red print (1, 2, 3 and 4)
twenty	Template F pieces, natural
twenty	Template G pieces, natural
five	Template H pieces, each red print (1, 2, 3 and 4)
five	Template I pieces, each red print (1, 2, 3 and 4)
twenty	Template J pieces, natural
twenty	Template K pieces, natural

Refer to Traditional Method for cutting borders.

Instructions:

1. For the First Section, make a strip-pieced fabric as follows: sew a 2 1/4" x 9" strip from natural, a 1 1/2" x 9" strip from red print, a 3 3/4" x 9" strip from natural, a 1 1/2" x 9" strip from same red print, and a 2 1/2" x 9" strip from natural, **Fig 2**. Cut crosswise at 1 1/2" intervals, **Fig 3**. You will need five sections from each red print.

2. Make Second Section, joining Template K, Template I, Template G, Template H and Template J pieces, **Fig 4**. You will need five sections from each red print.

3. For the Third Section, make three strip-pieced fabrics. For the first, sew a 1 1/2" strip from red print, a 2" strip from natural and a 1 1/2" strip from same red print. Cut crosswise at 4 1/2" intervals, **Fig 5**. You will need five from each red print. Attach Template C piece from red print to lower edge, **Fig 6**. Then attach Template F piece from natural to right edge, **Fig 7**.

For the second strip-pieced fabric, **Fig 8**, sew a 1" strip from natural and a 1" strip from red print. Cut crosswise at 5 1/2" intervals. You will need five pieces from each red print.

For the third strip-pieced fabric, sew a 1 1/2" strip from red print, a 1 1/2" strip from natural, a 1 1/2" strip from same red print, a 1 1/2" strip from natural, and a 1 1/2" strip from same red print, **Fig 9**. Cut crosswise at 3 1/2" intervals. You will need five from each red print.

Join the second and third pieces, **Fig 10**, and add Template D piece from red print, **Fig 11**. Join pieces for Third Section, **Fig 12**.

4. Join the three sections to make finished block.

5. Follow steps 1 to 4 of Traditional Method to complete your quilt.

Quilting Suggestion:

Quilt around the windows, doors and roofs of each schoolhouse as shown in **Fig 13**.

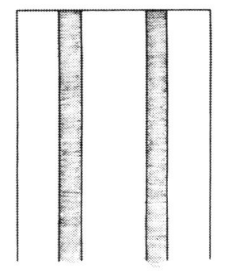

Fig 2

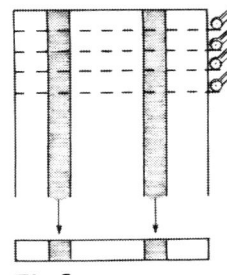

Fig 3 First Section

Fig 4 Second Section

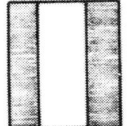

Fig 5 first strip-pieced fabric

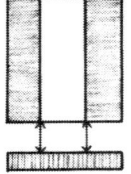

Fig 6

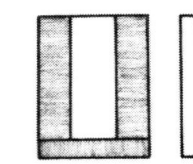

Fig 7

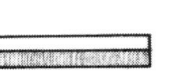

Fig 8 second strip-pieced fabric

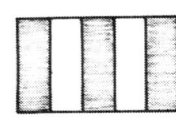

Fig 9 third strip-pieced fabric

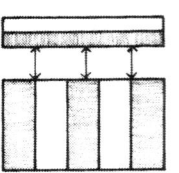

Fig 10

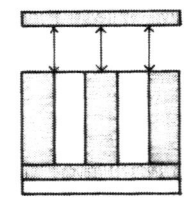

Fig 11

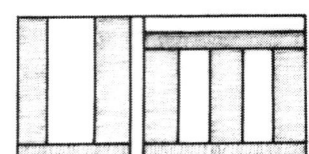

Fig 12 Third Section

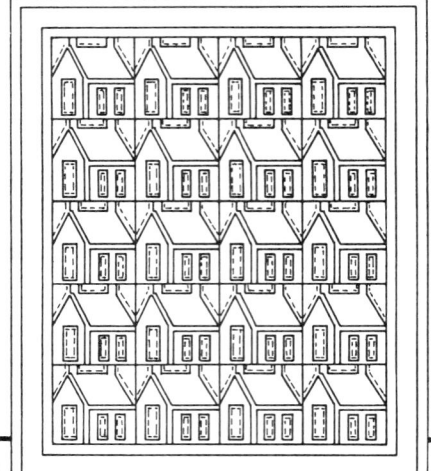

Fig 13

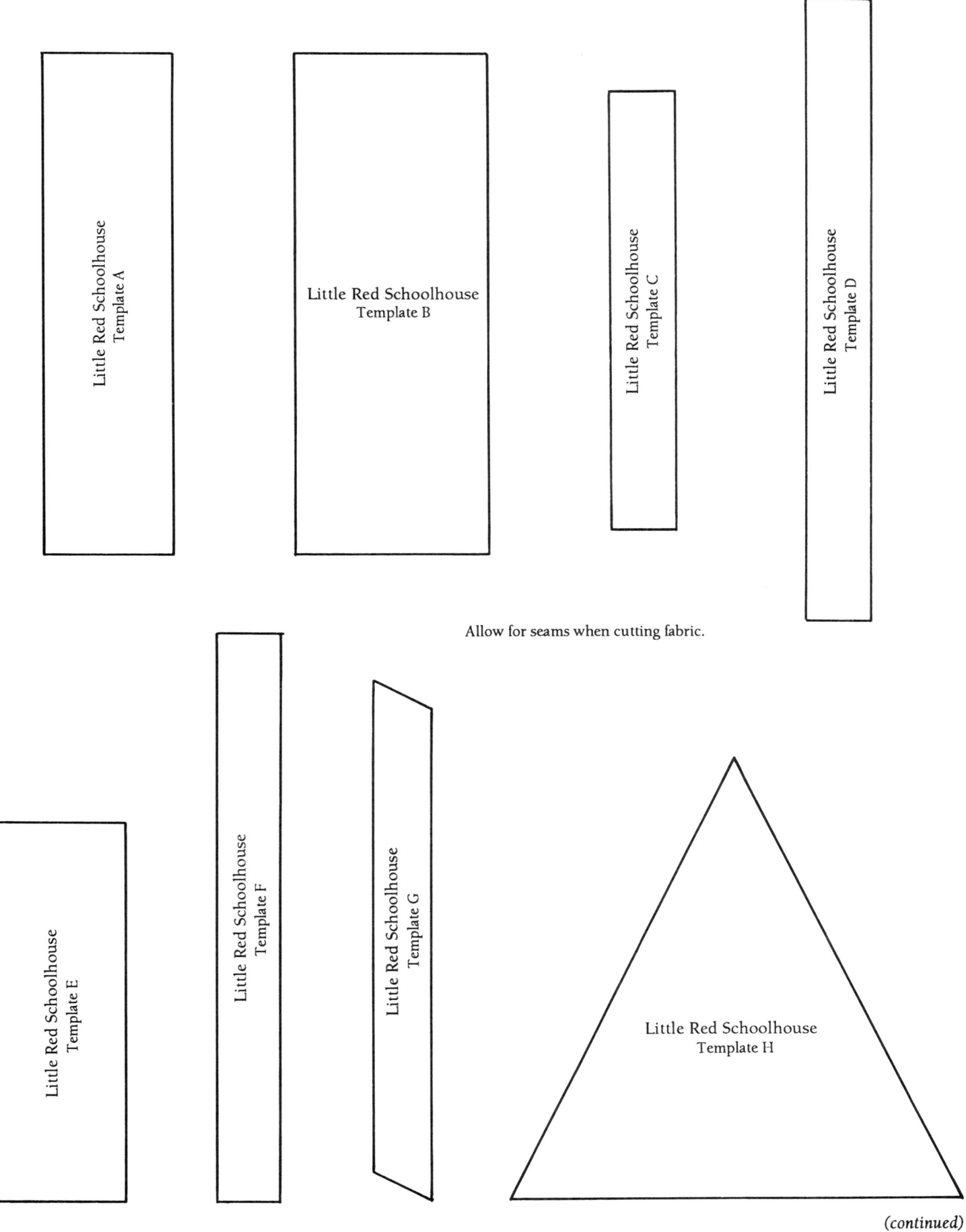

Allow for seams when cutting fabric.

(continued)

Little Red Schoolhouse

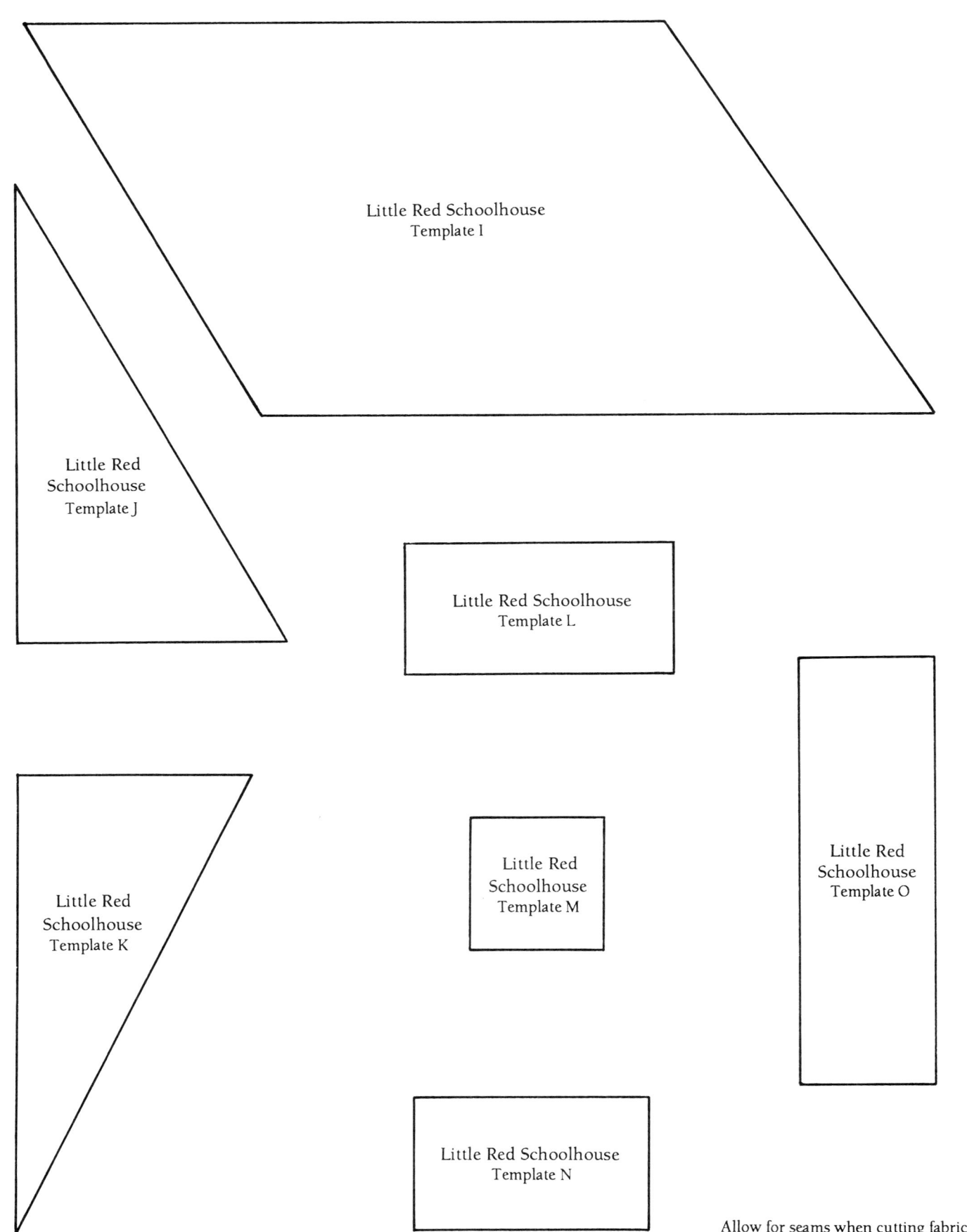

Allow for seams when cutting fabric.

Trip Around the Playground

Big Folks' Pattern: Trip Around the World

How big is a little child's world? Probably no bigger than his playground. So why not take a trip around and around the playground—especially when it is a quick and easy trip to make.

Size of Block:
2 1/2" x 2 1/2"

Size of Quilt:
Approx 52" x 52"

Setting:
The blocks are set 17 across and 17 down with a 1 1/2" dk blue border, a 2 1/2" lt blue border and a lt blue binding.

Fabric Requirements:
dk pink, lt pink fabric: 1/2 yd
dk blue fabric: 3/4 yds
lt blue fabric: 3 yds
    (includes backing and binding)

Traditional Method
Cut the following:
Template A lt pink   73
Template A dk pink   72
Template A dk blue   72
Template A lt blue   72

First Border:
Cut 2 dk blue strips, each 2" x 43" for sides
Cut 2 dk blue strips, each 2" x 46" for top and bottom

Second Border:
Cut 2 lt blue strips, each 3" x 46" for sides
Cut 2 lt blue strips, each 3" x 51" for top and bottom

Instructions:

1. Join the blocks following the quilt layout.

2. Add the dk blue border, and then add the lt blue border.

3. To finish quilt, follow instructions in *How to Make a Baby Quilt,* starting with Preparing the Quilt Top on page 4.

For color photograph, see page 24.

(continued)

Trip Around the Playground

Modern Method

You will be making 16 unit blocks, **Fig 1**, for this method, plus one extra vertical and horizontal row in the middle of the quilt.

Cut five 3"-wide crosswise strips from each fabric. Cut one 3" square lt pink for center of quilt.

1. Sew strips together lengthwise making 3 sets of Set 1-2 and Set 3-4 and 2 sets of Set 2-3 and Set 4-1 as follows:
Set 1-2   lt pink and dk blue
Set 3-4   lt blue and dk pink
Set 2-3   dk blue and lt blue
Set 4-1   dk pink and lt pink

2. Sew strip sets together as follows for each row of the unit block:
Row 1   Set 1-2 to Set 3-4
Row 2   Set 2-3 to Set 4-1
Row 3   Set 3-4 to Set 1-2
Row 4   Set 4-1 to Set 2-3
(You will have extra Row sets to be used for the center horizontal and vertical rows).

3. Cut across sets at 3" intervals. sew the four rows together to form unit block. Repeat until you have 16 unit blocks.

4. Sew 4 unit blocks together making one section; repeat three times.

5. To make horizontal and vertical rows, sew two Row 1 sets together on short side (refer to layout) then repeat three more times. For long horizontal row, sew a Row 1 strip to each side of the pink square noting placement in layout.

6. Noting that each section is turned a quarter turn, sew a section to each side of a short vertical strip for upper half; repeat for lower half. Sew the two halves to each side of the horizontal strip.

7. To finish quilt, follow instructions in *How to Make a Baby Quilt*, starting with Preparing the Quilt Top on page 4.

Quilting Suggestions:

The quilt shown in the photograph was quilted diagonally through the dk pink and dk blue squares and along the dk blue border as shown in **Fig 2**.

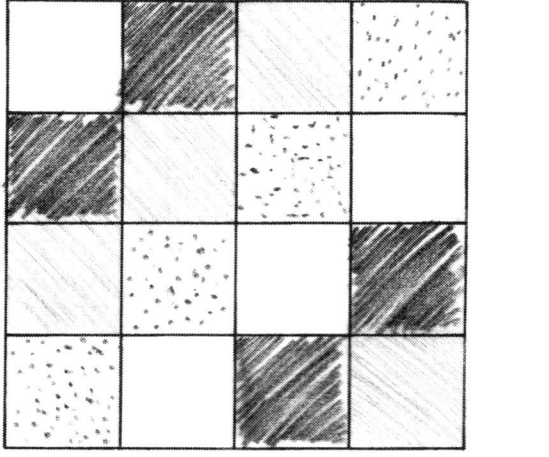
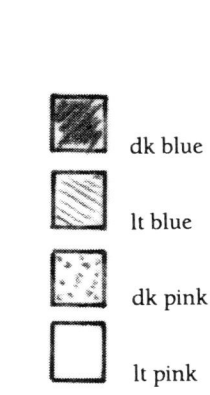

Fig 1 Unit Block

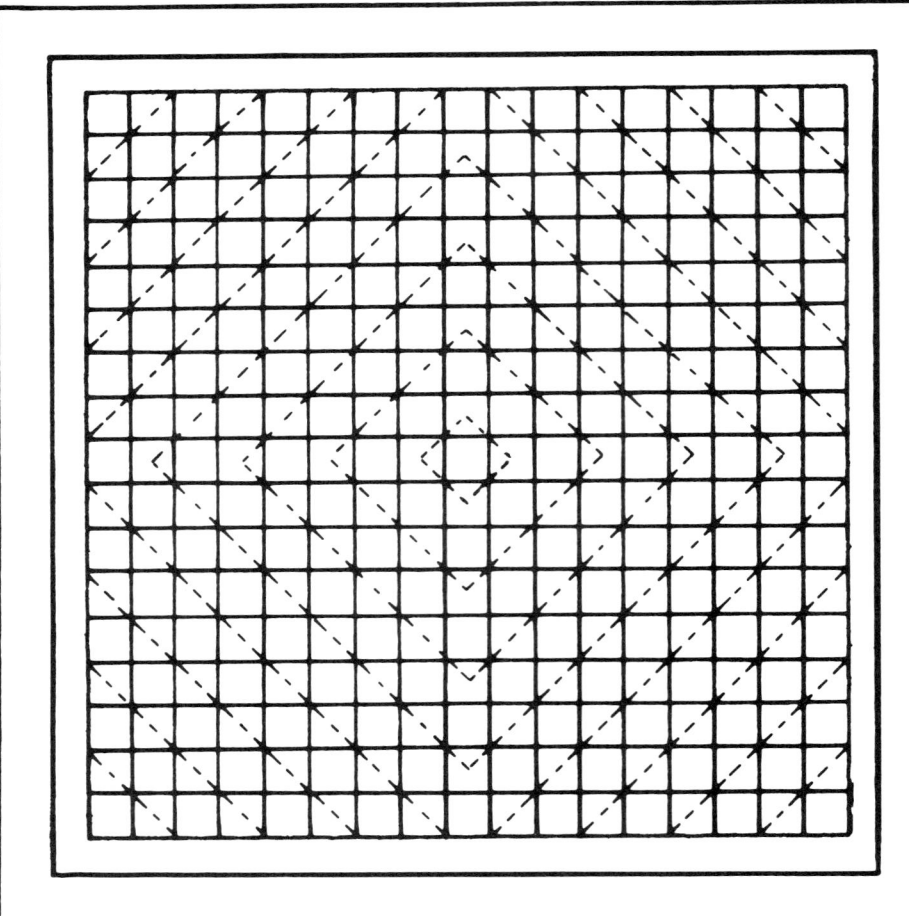

Fig 2 Trip Around the Playground Quilting Layout

Trip Around the Playground Layout

Trip Around the Playground
Template A

Allow for seams when cutting fabric.

Row, Row, Row Your Boat

Big Folks' Pattern: Sailboat

Row, row, row your boat gently down the stream. Merrily, merrily, merrily, merrily—life is but a dream. So dream on, little one, under this dreamy quilt.

Size of Block:
8" x 8"

Size of Quilt:
Approx 43 1/2" x 53 1/2"

Setting:
The blocks are set 4 across and 5 down with 2" sashing strips and squares created from Template A at the corners. The borders are made like the sashing strips and the quilt is finished with a 3/4" binding.

Fabric Requirements:
red, yellow, med blue fabric: 1/yd each
dk blue fabric: 3/4 yds
turquoise fabric: 2 3/4 yds (includes binding and backing)

Traditional Method
Cut the following:

Template	for block	for quilt
A turquoise	4	110
A red	2	40
A med blue	4	80
B yellow	4	80
B turquoise	6	120
B red	2	40

Sashing and Border Strips:
Cut 49 dk blue strips, each 8 1/2" x 2 1/2"

Instructions:

1. Make 20 blocks following the Block Diagram.

2. Join five blocks to sashing strips as shown in **Fig 1**. You now have a vertical strip of five joined blocks. Repeat for three more vertical strips.

3. Following **Fig 2**, create three sashing strips by joining four turquoise squares to five dark blue strips.

4. Following **Fig 3**, join the strips of blocks to the sashing strips.

5. Following **Fig 2**, create two additional strips to use as the side borders, and attach these side borders to each side.

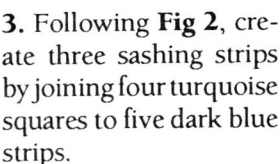
Fig 1

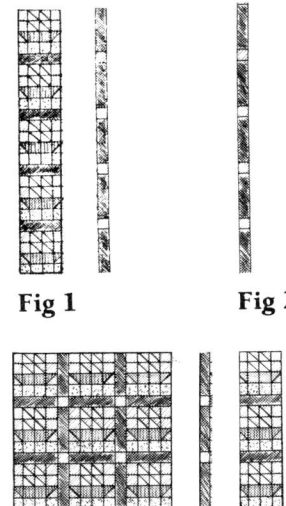
Fig 2

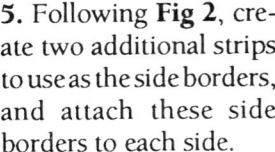
Fig 3

6. Following **Fig 4**, create the top and bottom borders from four dark blue strips and five turquoise squares. Attach these borders to the top and bottom of the quilt.

Fig 4

7. To finish quilt, follow instructions in *How to Make a Baby Quilt*, starting with Preparing the Quilt Top on page 4.

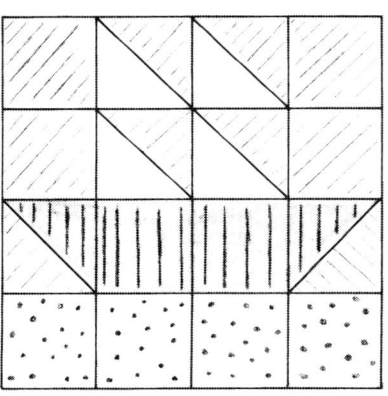
Block Diagram

- red
- yellow
- turquoise
- med blue
- dk blue

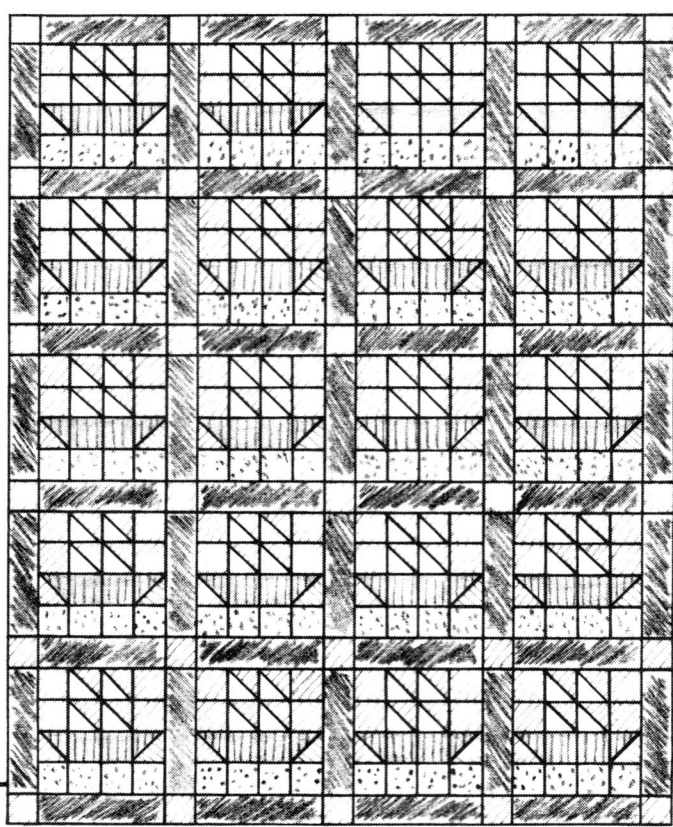
Row, Row, Row Your Boat Layout

For color photograph, see page 22.

(continued)

Modern Method

Cutting Requirements (strips cut crosswise):

one	18 1/4" x 21 1/4" piece, turquoise
one	18 1/4" x 21 1/4" piece, yellow
one	12 1/2" x 15 1/2" piece, turquoise
one	12 1/2" x 15 1/2" piece, red
four	2 1/2" strips, red
eight	2 1/2" strips, turquoise; cut two strips into thirty 2 1/2" squares
eight	2 1/2" strips, med blue
ten	2 1/2" strips, dk blue; cut strips into forty-nine 8 1/2" pieces

Instructions:

1. To make the turquoise/yellow pieced squares, follow these steps:

a. Starting at least 1/2" from all edges of wrong side of 18 1/4" x 21 1/4" yellow piece, draw a grid with lines 2 7/8" apart, being sure that your squares are drawn accurately. You will have a grid of six squares across and seven down, **Fig 5**.

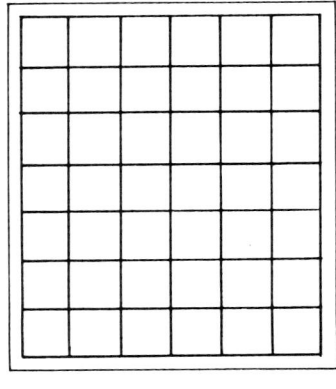
Fig 5

b. Draw diagonal lines through every other square, **Fig 6**.

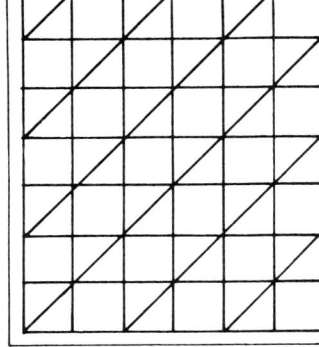
Fig 6

c. Draw diagonal lines in the opposite direction through all of the empty squares, **Fig 7**.

d. Place marked yellow piece right sides together with the 18 1/4" x 21 1/4" turquoise piece. Press together lightly and pin or baste the two pieces to hold in place. Referring to **Fig 8** and starting in a corner where the diagonal line goes from the outside to the inside of the square, stitch 1/4" to the left of the drawn diagonal line. Continue stitching along the diagonal lines until you reach the corner where you started. Make sure you have stitched on both sides of all diagonal lines.

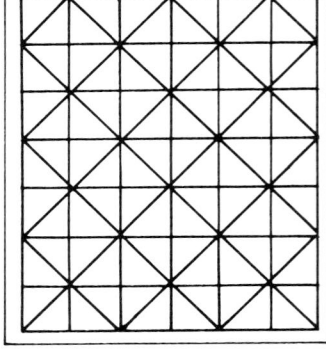
Fig 7

e. Remove pins or basting and press well. Using scissors or rotary cutter and mat, cut along every marked line - horizontal, vertical, and diagonal. You will have a total of 84 pieced squares; you will need 80 to complete your quilt. Press each pieced square open with the seam allowance toward the darker side. Clip "dog ears" from each square, **Fig 9**.

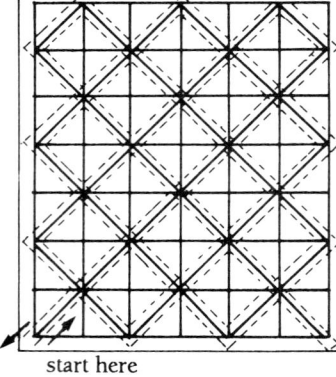
Fig 8

2. To make the turquoise/red pieced squares, follow these steps:

a. Starting at least 1/2" from all edges of wrong side of 12 1/2" x 15 1/2" turquoise piece, draw a grid with lines 2 7/8" apart, being sure that your squares are drawn accurately. You will have a grid of four squares across and five down.

b. Follow **Fig 10** and steps b to e above to make your pieced squares. You will have a total of 40 turquoise/red pieced squares.

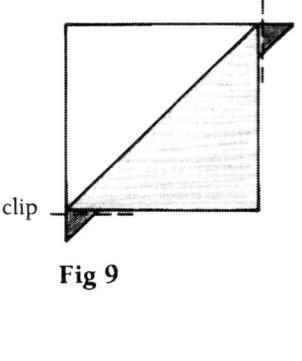
Fig 9

3. Sew two turquoise strips together lengthwise. Cut crosswise every 2 1/2", **Fig 11**. Repeat with four more strips until you have 40 sewn pairs of turquoise squares.

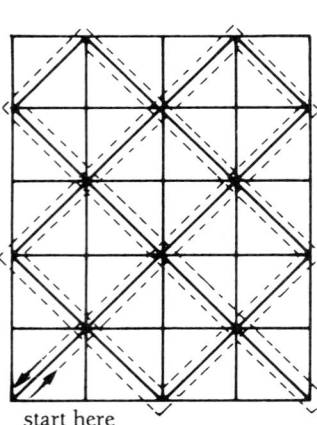
Fig 10

4. Sew two red strips together lengthwise. Cut crosswise every 2 1/2". Repeat with remaining strips until you have 20 sewn pairs of red squares.

5. Sew four med blue strips together lengthwise. Cut crosswise every 2 1/2", **Fig 12**. Repeat with remaining four strips until you have 20 sewn strips of med blue squares.

6. Following **Fig 13**, sew Sailboat Block together. Repeat until you have 20 Blocks.

7. Follow steps 2 to 7 of the Traditional Method above to finish your quilt.

Quilting Suggestion:
The quilt shown in the photograph was quilted around the sails and the boat. In addition, the quilting template was used along the sashing as shown in **Fig 14**.

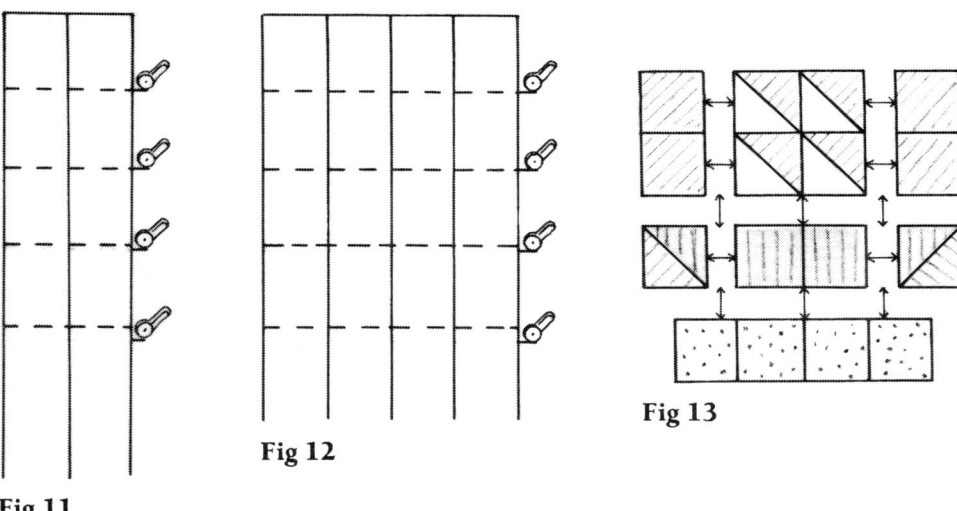

Fig 11

Fig 12

Fig 13

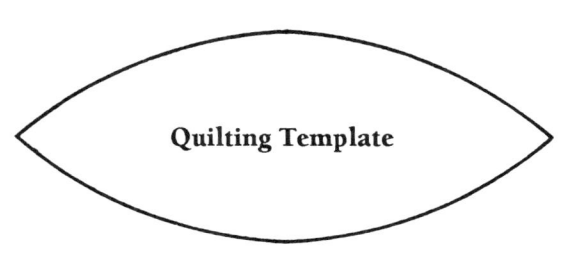

Quilting Template

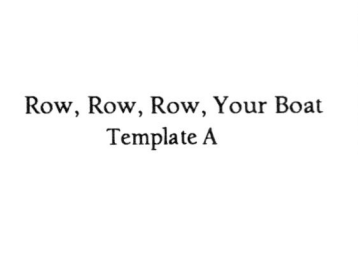

Row, Row, Row, Your Boat
Template A

Allow for seams when cutting fabric.

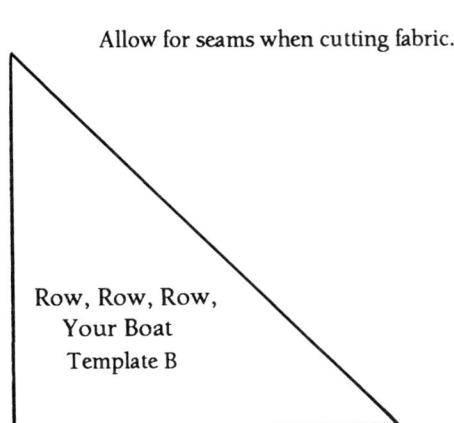

Row, Row, Row, Your Boat
Template B

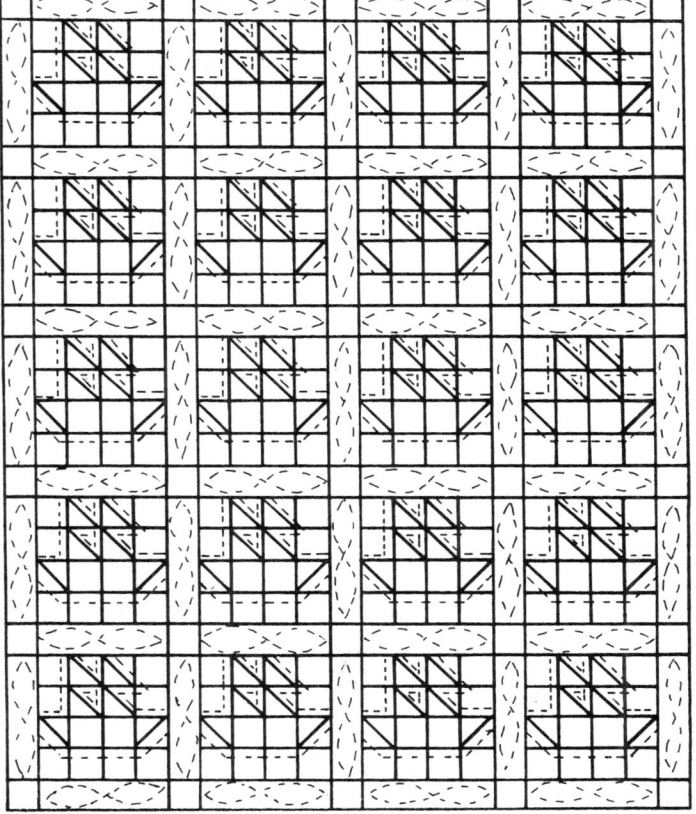

Fig 14 Row, Row, Row Your Boat Quilting Layout

Regular size Coverlet 78 x 92

Crayons

Big Folks' Pattern: Rail Fence

In keeping with our theme of taking traditional patterns and changing them for little folks, we decided to turn a "Rail Fence" into "Playpen Fence". However, when the quilt was completed, its bright colors made us think of those colorful crayons we played with as children.

Size of Block:
9" x 9"

Size of Quilt:
Approx 43 1/2" x 52 1/2"

Setting:
The blocks are set 4 across and 5 down with a 3" border and a 3/4" binding.

Fabric Requirements:

yellow, orange, purple, blue, green fabric:	1/2 yd
red fabric:	3 1/4 yds (includes border, backing and binding)

Traditional Method
Cut the following:

Template A red	20
Template A yellow	20
Template A orange	20
Template A purple	20
Template A blue	20
Template A green	20

Side Borders:
Cut two red strips, each 3 1/2" x 45 1/2"

Top and Bottom Borders:
Cut two red strips, each 3 1/2" x 42 1/2

Instructions:

1. Following the Block Diagram, make 20 blocks following the same color sequence in each block.

2. Following the Quilt Layout, join the blocks.

3. Add the red borders to sides and then to top and bottom.

4. To finish quilt, follow finishing instructions in *How to Make a Baby Quilt*, starting with Preparing the Quilt Top on page 4.

Modern Method
Cutting Requirements:

five	2" strips (cut crosswise), red, yellow, orange, purple, blue and green
two	3 1/2" x 45 1/2" strips, red for side borders
two	3 1/2" x 42 1/2" strips, red for top and bottom borders.

Instructions:

1. Sew one strip of each color in the order shown in Block Diagram. Repeat with remaining strips until you have five strip-pieced fabrics.

2. Cut crosswise every 9 1/2", **Fig 1**, until you have 20 blocks.

3. Repeat steps 2 to 4 of Traditional Method to complete the quilt.

Quilting Suggestions:
The photographed quilt was quilted in the ditch around each of the crayons.

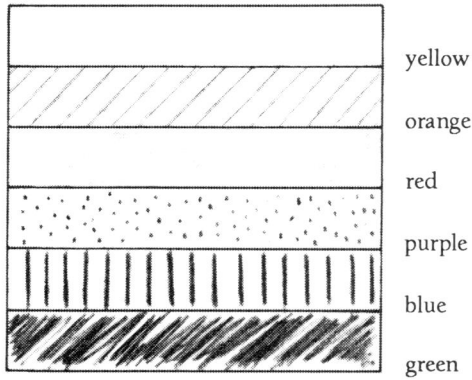

Block Diagram

(colors top to bottom: yellow, orange, red, purple, blue, green)

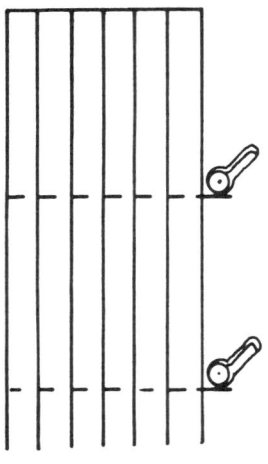

Fig 1

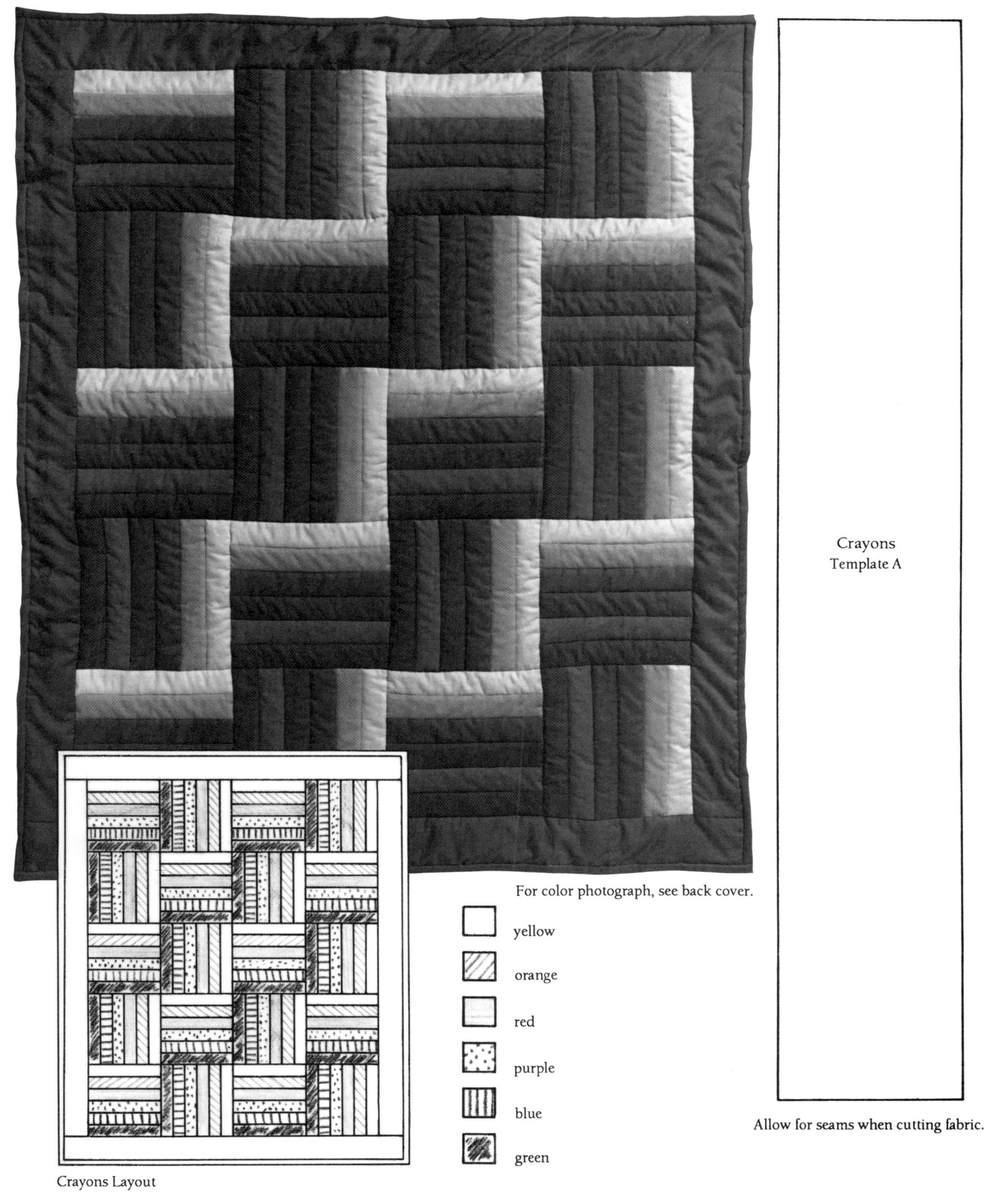

Crayons
Template A

For color photograph, see back cover.

- ☐ yellow
- ▨ orange
- ▤ red
- ⋯ purple
- ▦ blue
- ▩ green

Allow for seams when cutting fabric.

Crayons Layout

Teddy Bear Paws

Big Folks' Pattern: Bear's Paw

A big bear on a bed would scare anyone--especially with all those claws! But an adorable teddy bear is a wonderful companion for any child drifting off to dreamland. And when that special child awakens, he finds the tracks of his teddy bear parading across his quilt.

Size of Block:
7" x 7"

Size of Quilt:
Approx 48 1/2" x 66 1/2"

Setting:
The blocks are set 5 across and 6 down with 2" sashing strips between the blocks and a 2" border and a 3/4" binding.

Fabric Requirements:
red fabric: 4 1/2 yds (includes border)
white fabric: 4 1/2 yds (includes backing and binding)

Traditional Method
Cut the following:

	for block	for quilt
Template A red	16	480
Template A white	16	480
Template B red	1	30
Template B white	4	120
Template C white	4	120
Template D red	4	120

Block Sashing Strips:
Cut 25 red strips each 2 1/2" x 7 1/2"

Long Sashing Strips:
Cut 4 red strips each 2 1/2" x 52 1/2"

Side Borders:
Cut 2 red strips each 2 1/2" x 52 1/2"

Top and Bottom Borders:
Cut 2 red strips each 2 1/2" x 47 1/2"

Instructions:

1. Make 30 blocks following the Block Diagram.

2. Join five block sashing strips to six blocks as shown in **Fig 1**. You now have a vertical strip of six joined blocks.

3. Make four more vertical strips.

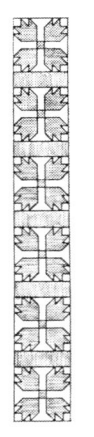   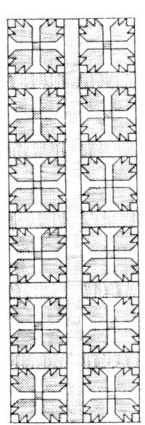

Fig 1   Fig 2

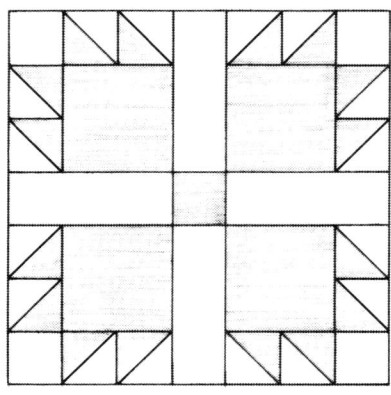

Block Diagram

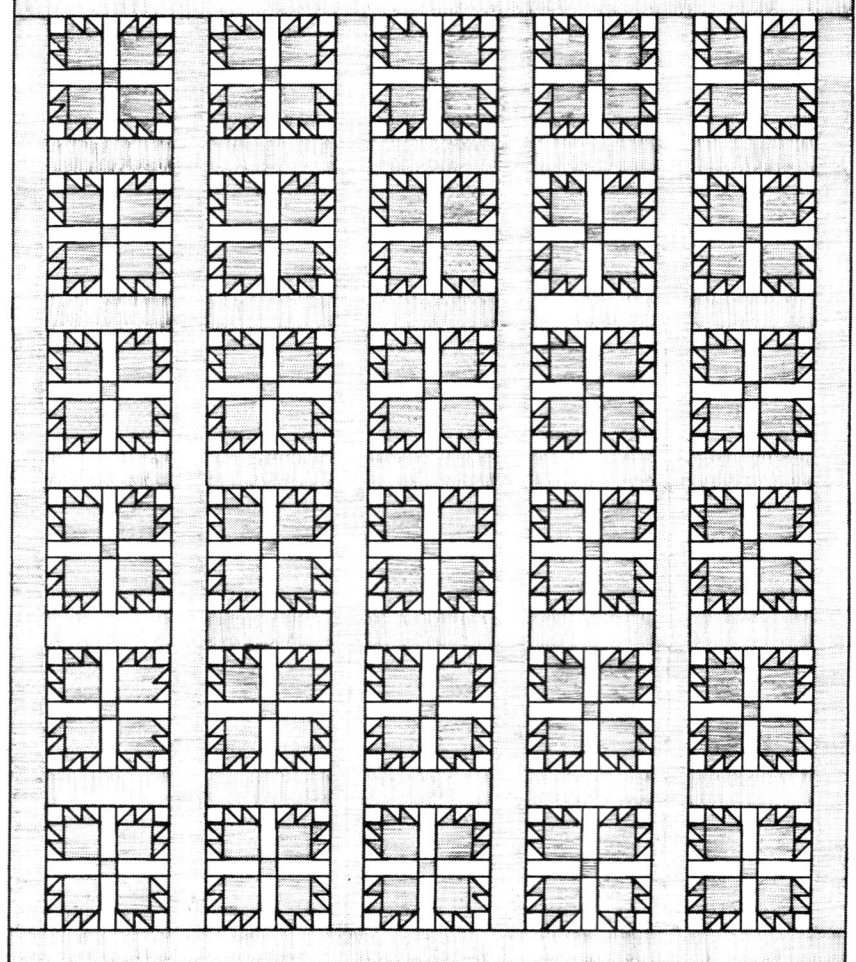

Teddy Bear Paws Layout

34

4. Join the vertical strips together with the side sashing strip as in **Fig 2**.

5. Add side borders. Add top and bottom borders.

6. To finish quilt, follow instructions in *How to Make a Baby Quilt*, starting with Preparing the Quilt Top on page 4.

Modern Method
Cut the following for blocks (crosswise):
6 red pieces each 12 1/4" x 15"
6 white pieces each 12 1/4" x 15"
120 white strips each 3 1/2" x 1 1/2"
thirty 1 1/2" red squares
eight 2 1/2" red strips

Cut Block Sashing, Long Sashing, Side Borders and Top and Bottom Borders as for Traditional Method above.

Instructions:
To make the pieced squares, use the 12 1/4" x 15" pieces of red and white fabrics and follow these steps:

1. Starting at least 1/2" from all edges of **wrong** side of white piece, draw a grid with lines 1 7/8" apart, being sure that your squares are drawn **accurately**, **Fig 3**. You will have a grid of six squares across and seven squares down.

2. Draw diagonal lines through every other square, **Fig 4**.

3. Draw diagonal lines in the opposite direction through all of the empty squares, **Fig 5**.

4. Place marked white piece right sides together with a red piece. Press together lightly and pin or baste the two pieces to hold in place. Referring to **Fig 6** and starting in a corner where the diagonal line goes from the outside to the inside, stitch 1/4" to the left of the drawn diagonal line. Continue stitching along the diagonal lines until you reach the corner where you started. Make sure you have stitched on both sides of all diagonal lines.

5. Remove pins or basting and press well. Using scissors or rotary cutter and mat, cut along every marked line—horizontal, vertical, and diagonal. Press each pieced square open with the seam allowance toward the darker side. Clip "dog ears" from each square, **Fig 7**.

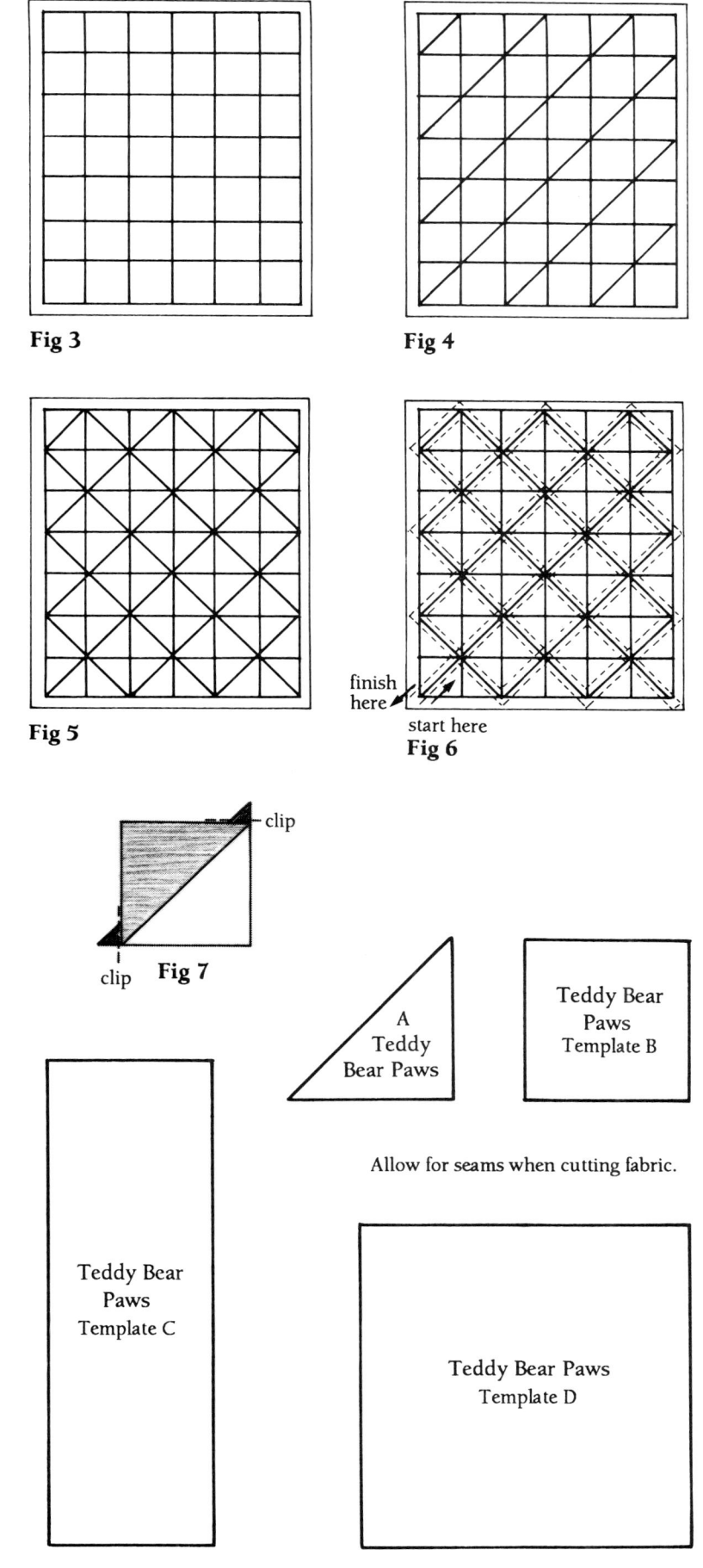

Allow for seams when cutting fabric.

(continued)

Teddy Bear Paws

Separate the pieced squares as in **Fig 8** with 240 in each stack. Using pieced squares from first stack, **Fig 9**, stitch two squares right sides together and continue to chain piece, **Fig 10**, until there are 120 pairs of pieced squares, **Fig 11**. Clip thread between pairs. Repeat for second stack.

Taking a 1 1/2" white strip, chain piece with pairs from first stack, **Fig 12**. Repeat until all pairs are chain pieced to a white strip. Carefully, cut between each pair, **Fig 13**. Press open to form Unit 1, **Fig 14**.

Using a 2 1/2" red strip, chain piece with pairs from second stack, **Fig 15**. Repeat until all of pairs are chain pieced to a red strip. Carefully cut between pairs. Press open to form Unit 2, **Fig 16**.

Sew a Unit 1 to a Unit 2, **Fig 17**, forming Unit 3. Chain piece the remaining Unit 1 and Unit 2 pieces for a total of 120 Unit 3.

Attach a Unit 3 to each side of a 1 1/2" x 3 1/2" white strip for Unit 4, **Fig 18**. You will have 60 Unit 4.

Sew short end of a 1 1/2" x 3 1/2" white strip to a 1 1/2" red square to complete Unit 5, **Fig 19**. You will have 30 Unit 5.

Using two Unit 4 and one Unit 5, assemble block as in Block Diagram on page 34.

Refer to steps 2 through 6 of Traditional Method to finish your quilt.

Quilting Suggestion:
The quilt shown in the photograph was quilted around the "paws" as shown in **Fig 20**.

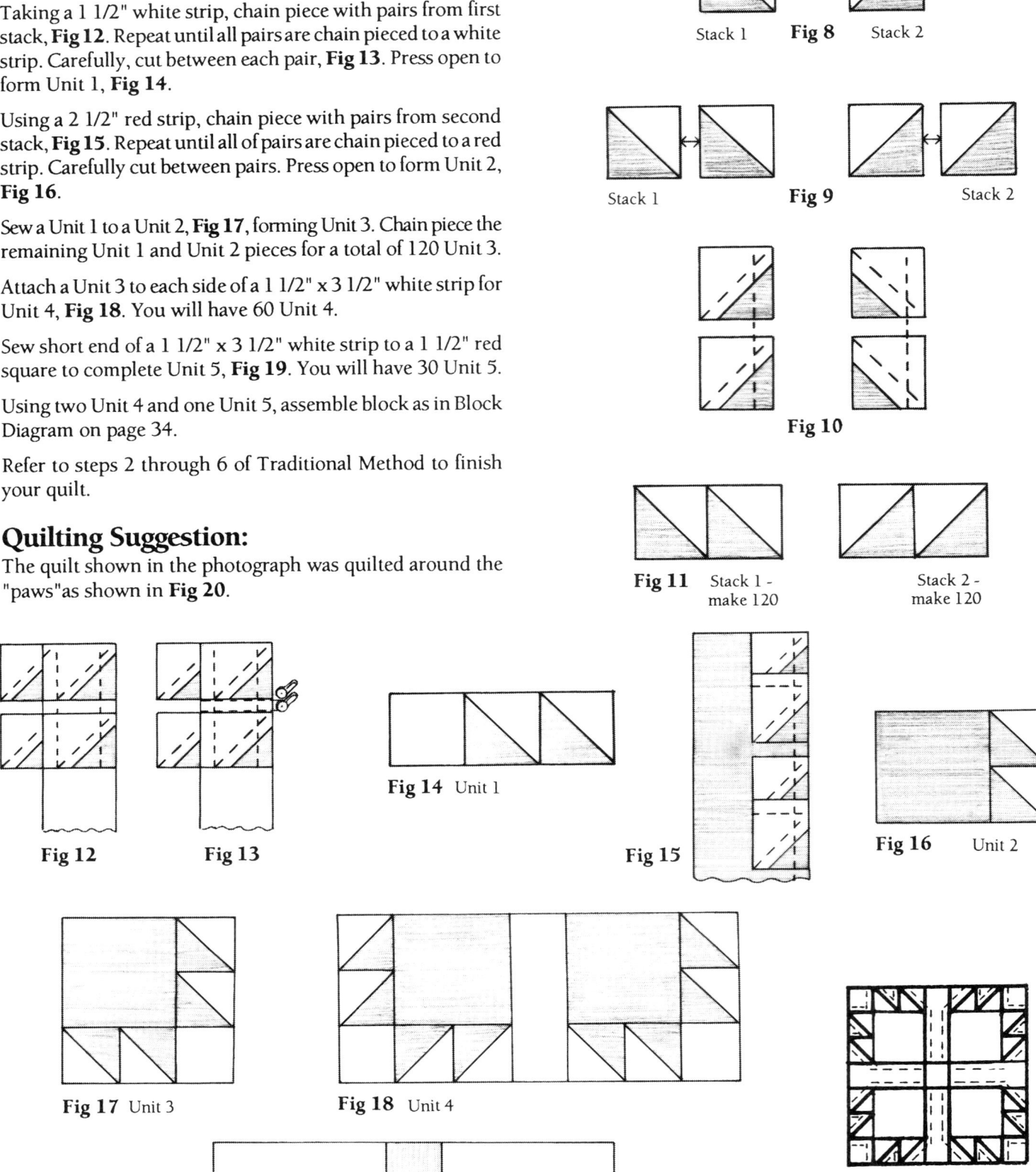

For color photograph, see page 22.

Sunshine to Scare Away The Shadows

Big Folks' Pattern: Sunshine and Shadow

At night there are lots of scary shadows that creep into a little one's bedroom. Sleeping under this sunny quilt, however, is a sure way to keep those scary shadows from disturbing a restful night.

Size of Block:
3" x 3"

Size of Quilt:
Approx 39 1/2" x 48 1/2"

Setting:
The blocks are set 13 across and 16 down with a 3/4" binding.

Fabric Requirements:
dk rust, yellow print,
yellow: 1/2 yd
peach: 2 yds (includes backing and binding)

Traditional Method

Cut the following:

Template A dk rust (1)	52
Template A peach (2)	52
Template A yellow print(3)	52
Template A yellow(4)	52

1. Join the blocks following the Quilt Layout.

2. To finish quilt, follow instructions in *How to Make a Baby Quilt*, starting with Preparing the Quilt Top on page 4.

Modern Method

You will be making 12 unit blocks, **Fig 1**, for this method plus an extra vertical row along the right side.

Cut 5 crosswise strips 3 1/2" wide of each of the 4 fabrics.

1. Sew strips together lengthwise making 3 sets of Set 1/2 and Set 3/4 and 2 sets of Set 2/3 and Set 4/1 as follows:

   Set 1/2 - dk rust + peach
   Set 3/4 - yellow print + yellow
   Set 2/3 - peach + yellow print
   Set 4/1 - yellow + dk rust

2. Sew strip sets together as follows for each row of the unit block.

   Row 1 - Set 1/2 to Set 3/4
   Row 2 - Set 2/3 to Set 4/1
   Row 3 - Set 3/4 to Set 1/2
   Row 4 - Set 4/1 to Set 2/3

(You will have an extra Row 1 set to be used for the vertical row on the right edge of the quilt layout.)

3. Cut across sets at 3 1/2" intervals. Sew the four Rows together to form unit blocks. Repeat until you have 12 unit blocks. Sew extra Row 1 sets together vertically for row on right edge.

4. Join the blocks following the Quilt Layout.

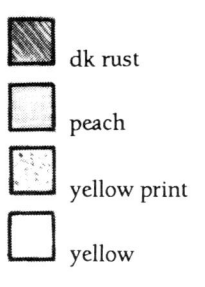

- dk rust
- peach
- yellow print
- yellow

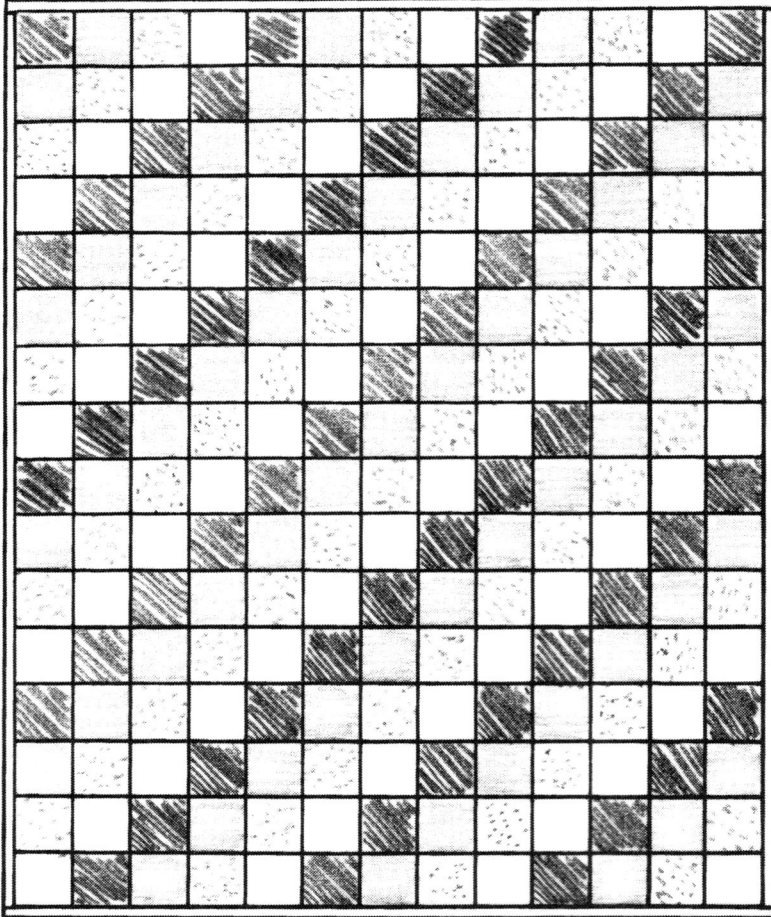

Sunshine to Scare Away the Shadows Layout

5. To finish quilt, follow instructions in *How to Make a Baby Quilt*, starting with Preparing the Quilt Top on page 4.

Quilting Suggestion:
The quilt shown in the photograph was quilted diagonally through each square as shown in **Fig 2**.

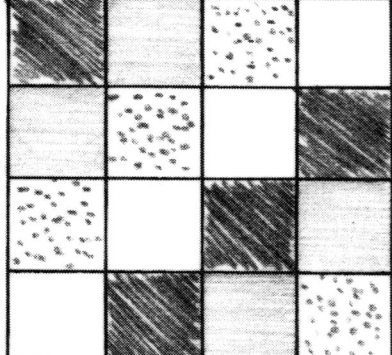

Fig 1 Unit Block

For color photograph, see page 21.

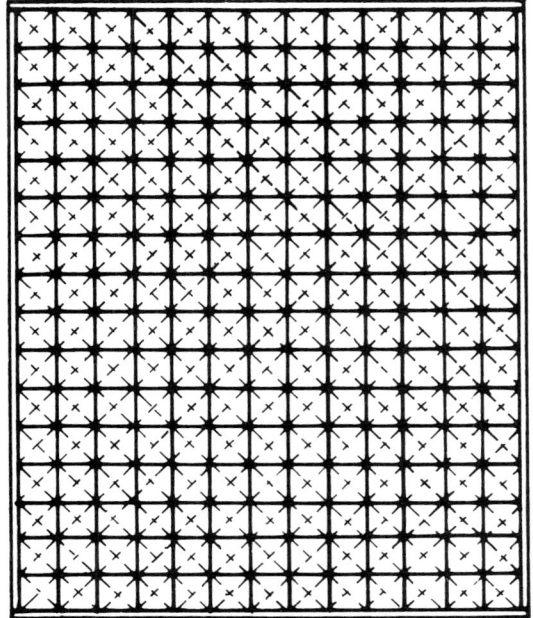

Fig 2 Quilting Layout

Sunshine to Scare Away the Shadows
Template A

Allow for seams when cutting fabric.

Little Irish Leprechaun

Big Folks' Pattern: Double Irish Chain

You don't have to be a little colleen to enjoy this quilt. Any little pixie would love to sleep under this cover that has been quilted with 40 sweet little hearts.

Size of Block:
10" x 10"

Size of Quilt:
Approx 41 1/2" x 51 1/2"

Setting:
The blocks are set 4 across and 5 down with 3/4" binding of the print fabric.

Fabric Requirements:
pink fabric: 2 1/4 yds
print fabric: 3 1/4 yds (includes backing and binding)

Traditional Method
Cut the following:

	for block	for quilt
Template A pink	26	520
Template A print	32	640
Template B pink	8	160
Template C pink	2	40

Instructions:

1. Make 20 blocks following Block Diagram.

2. Join blocks following Quilt Layout.

3. To finish quilt, follow instructions in *How to Make a Baby Quilt*, starting with Preparing the Quilt Top on page 4.

Modern Method

You will be making 20 unit blocks as in Block Diagram for this method. Each unit block, will have two squares each of Blocks 1 and 2.

Cutting Requirements:
29 crosswise strips 1 1/2" wide from pink
25 crosswise strips 1 1/2" wide from print
7 crosswise strips 3 1/2" wide from pink

Instructions:

1. For Block 1, sew three 1 1/2" pink strips and two 1 1/2" print strips lengthwise alternating fabrics; see Piece I in **Fig 1**. Sew three 1 1/2" print strips and two 1 1/2" pink strips lengthwise alternating fabrics; see Piece II in **Fig 1**.

2. Cut 1 1/2" strips across the sewn strips; sew strips together making 40 Block 1's, **Fig 2**.

3. For Block 2, sew a 1 1/2" pink strip lengthwise on each side of a 3 1/2" pink strip; see Piece III in **Fig 3** Cut at 3 1/2" intervals. Repeat until you have 40 pieces. Sew a 1 1/2" print strip lengthwise on each side of a 3 1/2" pink strip; see Piece IV in **Fig 4**. Cut at 1 1/2" intervals. Repeat until you have 80 pieces. Sew pieces making 40 Block 2's, **Fig 5**.

4. Sew 20 unit blocks following Block Diagram.

5. To finish quilt, follow instructions in *How to Make a Baby Quilt*, starting with Preparing the Quilt Top on page 4.

Quilting Suggestion:

Using the quilting template, quilt the little heart in the 3" squares.

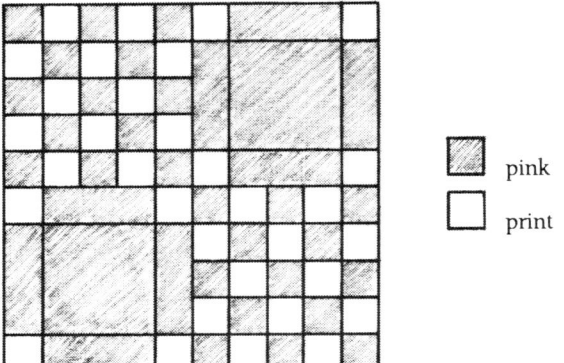

Block Diagram

Little Irish Leprechaun Layout

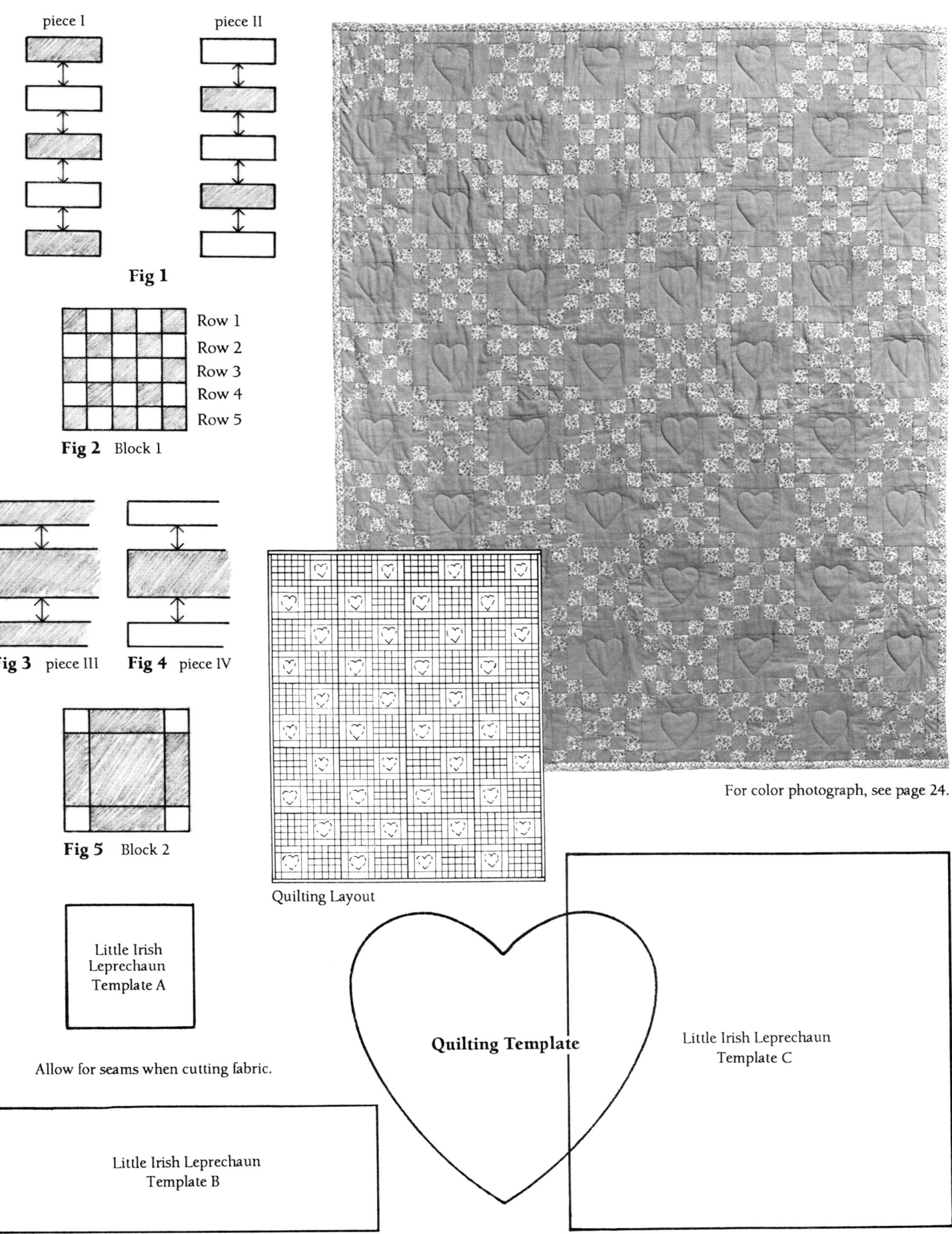

Fig 1

Fig 2 Block 1

Fig 3 piece III **Fig 4** piece IV

Fig 5 Block 2

Little Irish Leprechaun Template A

Allow for seams when cutting fabric.

Little Irish Leprechaun Template B

Quilting Layout

Quilting Template

Little Irish Leprechaun Template C

For color photograph, see page 24.

A Tisket A Tasket
Big Folks' Pattern: Basketweave

A green and pink basket is perfect for any child's room, and this quilt would please any mother and any child. We've used four different pink fabrics to add interest to the quilt. You may prefer to use only one.

Size of Block:
9" x 9"

Size of Quilt:
Approx 45 1/2" x 54 1/2"

Setting:
The blocks are set 4 across and 5 down with a 4" border and a 3/4" binding made from the green fabric.

Fabric Requirements:
four pink fabrics: 1/2 yd. each
green fabric: 3 yds (includes borders, backing and binding)

Traditional Method
Cut the Following:

	Template A
pink 1	10
pink 2	10
pink 3	10
pink 4	10
green	20

Side borders:
Cut two green strips, each 4 1/2" x 45 1/2"

Top and Bottom Borders:
Cut two green strips, each 4 1/2" x 36 1/2"

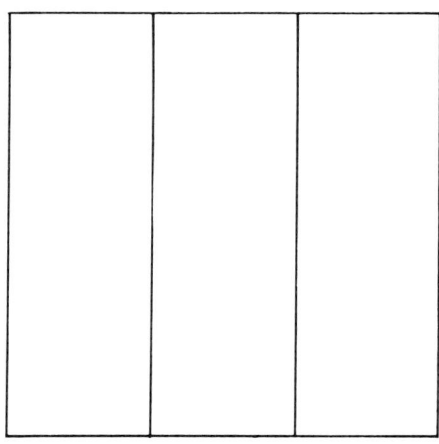

Block Diagram

Instructions:
1. Following the Block Diagram make 10 blocks using pink 1, pink 2 and green fabrics and 10 blocks using pink 3, pink 4, and green fabrics.

2. Following the Quilt Layout, join the blocks to make quilt.

3. Join border strips to sides first and then to top and bottom.

4. To finish quilt, follow instructions in *How to Make a Baby Quilt*, starting with Preparing the Quilt Top on page 4.

Modern Method
Cutting Requirements (crosswise):
three   3 1/2" strips from each of four pink prints 1, 2, 3 and 4
six   3 1/2" strips from green print

Cut Side Borders and Top and Bottom Borders as specified in Traditional Method above.

1. For Block A, **Fig 1**, join a pink 1, green print and pink 2 strip. Repeat with remaining strips until you have 3 strip-pieced fabrics. For Block B, **Fig 2**, join a pink 3, green print and pink 4 strip. Repeat with remaining strips until you have three strip-pieced fabrics.

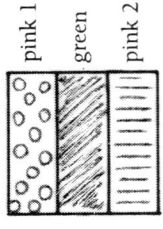 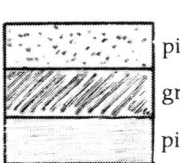

Fig 1 Block A   Fig 2 Block B

2. Cut crosswise every 9 1/2" along strip-pieced fabrics, **Fig 3**, until you have 10 each of Block A and Block B.

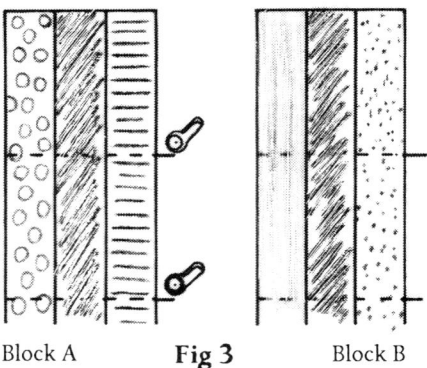

Block A   Fig 3   Block B

3. Follow steps 2 to 4 of Traditional Method above to complete your quilt.

Quilting Suggestion:
The photographed quilt was quilted in the ditch around all of the pieces.

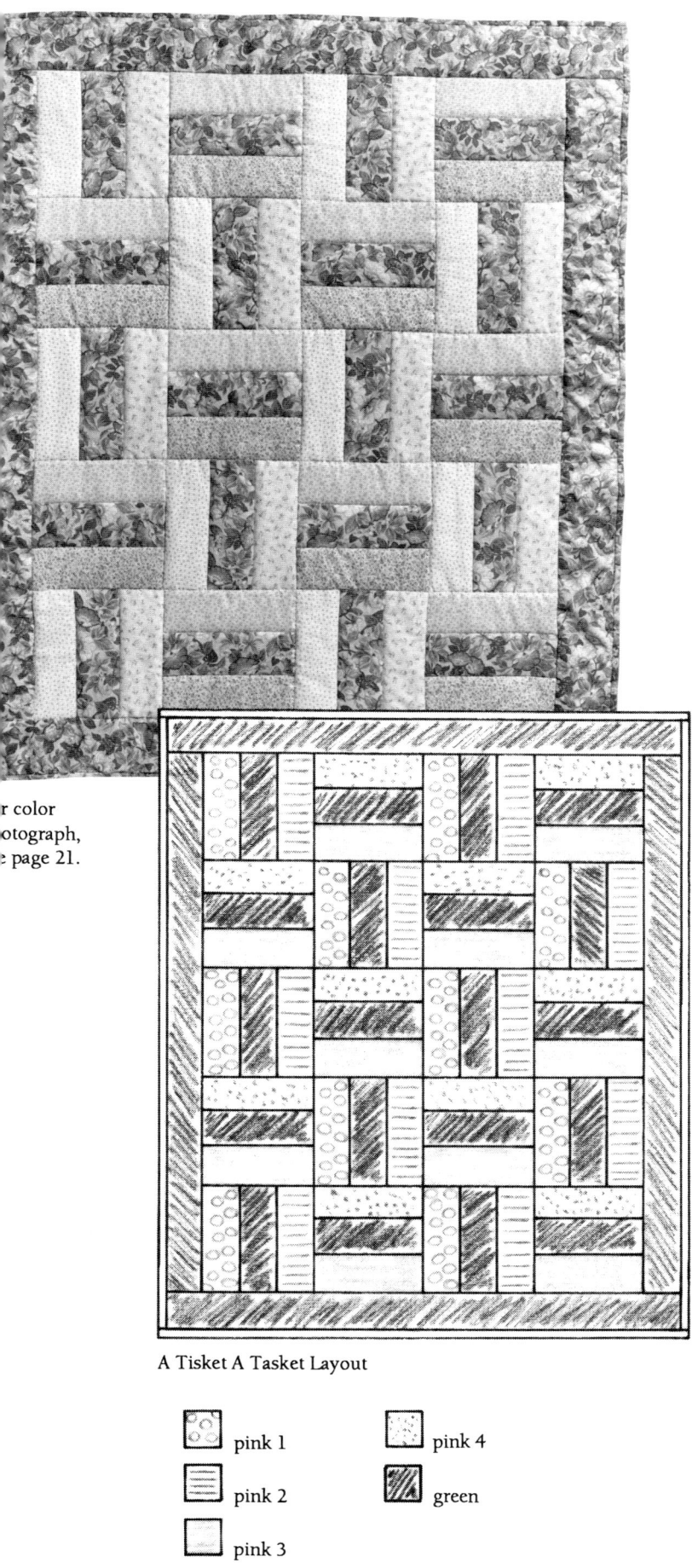

A Tisket A Tasket Layout

- pink 1
- pink 2
- pink 3
- pink 4
- green

A Tisket A Tasket
Template A

Kites Flying

Big Folks' Pattern: Kaleidoscope

It's a cold and blustery day; kites are flying in the air. But our little folk is asleep in his toasty-warm bed; the only kites flying for him are the ones flying across his quilt.

Size of Block:
8" x 8"

Size of Quilt:
Approx 41 1/2" x 41 1/2"

Setting:
The blocks are set 5 across and 5 down. The quilt is finished with a 3/4" binding made of the natural fabric.

Fabric Requirements:
yellow, green, lt blue, orange: 1/4 yd
dk blue, purple, pink, red: 1/2 yd
natural: 2 yds (includes backing and binding)

Traditional Method
Cut the following from Templates A, B, C, and D:

	A	B	C	D
yellow	10	10		
green	6	6		
lt blue	10	10		
dk blue	14	14		
purple	18	18		
pink	18	18		
red	14	14		
orange	10	10		
natural			100	100

Instructions:

Note: There are nine different color combinations of blocks. Fig 1 shows you how many of each to make.

1. Make the blocks following the Block Diagram.

2. Join the blocks into rows following the Quilt Layout.

3. To finish quilt, follow instructions in *How to Make a Baby Quilt*, starting with Preparing the Quilt Top on page 4.

Quilting Suggestion:
The photographed quilt was quilted around the "Kites" as shown in **Fig 2**.

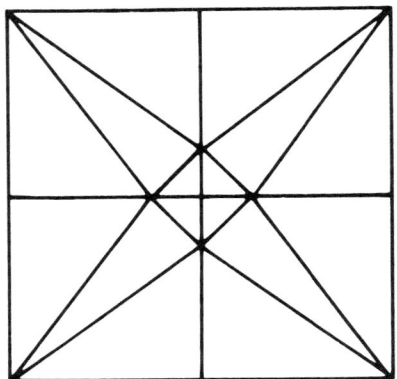

Block Diagram

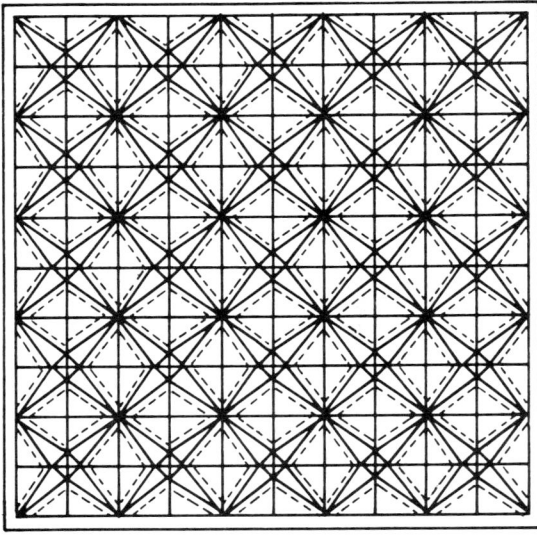

Fig 2 Quilting Layout

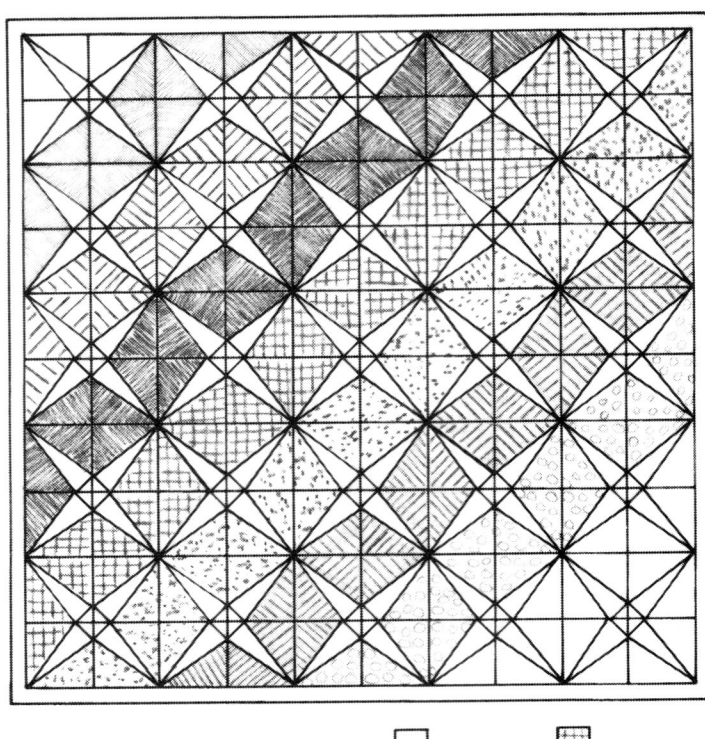

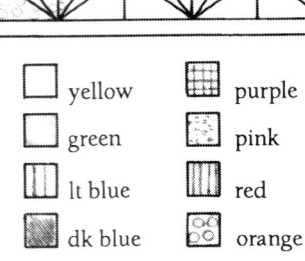